Amy Lowell

Twayne's United States Authors Series

David J. Nordloh, Editor

Indiana University, Bloomington

TUSAS 483

AMY LOWELL in 1922

Amy Lowell

By Richard Benvenuto

Michigan State University

Twayne Publishers • Boston

Amy Lowell

Richard Benvenuto

Copyright © 1985 by G.K. Hall & Company
All Rights Reserved
Published by Twayne Publishers
A Division of G.K. Hall & Company
70 Lincoln Street
Boston, Massachusetts 02111

Book Production by Elizabeth Todesco
Book Design by Barbara Anderson

Printed on permanent/durable acid-free
paper and bound in the United States of
America.

Library of Congress Cataloging in Publication Data

Benvenuto, Richard.
    Amy Lowell.

    (Twayne's United States authors series; TUSAS 483)
    Bibliography: p. 155
    Includes index.
    1. Lowell, Amy, 1874-1925—Criticism and interpretation.
I. Title   II. Series
PS3523.088Z58   1985   811'.52   85-5433
ISBN 0-8057-7436-X

Contents

About the Author

Richard Benvenuto, professor of English at Michigan State University, has published articles on Charlotte Brontë, Robert Browning, Ernest Dowson, Dickinson, Keats, and Hardy. He is also the author of *Emily Brontë,* a volume in the Twayne English Authors Series.

Preface

Although it has been sixty years since Amy Lowell died, there is still not an adequate, ample criticism of her poetry. Most of the important work on her has been biographical—particularly the detailed, informative biography by S. Foster Damon, to which my own chapter on her life is indebted. Some of Lowell's letters have been published, and there are numerous memoirs and reminiscences by friends and colleagues. She occupied a chapter—or the large part of a chapter—in the lives of many who were writing, reviewing, or printing poetry in the first decades of this century. But her own poetry, although it has not been entirely neglected, is often judged (and dismissed) without having been given a fair hearing. G. R. Ruihley's is the only serious book-length study of Lowell's poetry that I have been able to find, and there has not been a profusion of critical articles. Though she was a dominant figure in the New Poetry years, a prolific and popular writer of poetry and prose who by now ought to be a subject for revaluation, Lowell has still to receive the primary evaluation that she deserves.

My aim has been to give Lowell a fair and detailed reading, to suggest the scope and limitations of her art, and to acquaint the reader with poems that ought not to be neglected any longer. I am as aware as anyone can be that Lowell wrote many mediocre poems—so, as a matter of fact, did Hardy and Lawrence. I discuss some of Lowell's failures. But I am also convinced that poems like "Written on the Reverse," "Anecdote," and "The Doll," which I have not found in any recent anthology or classroom text, ought to be in such books and made more easily available to students and scholars. Even if Lowell is not the equal of Hardy or Lawrence, she wrote a number of poems that are worthy of serious assessment, that show she was a genuine poet. Even her failures are often interesting. What seem to be the most widespread and prevailing images of her—Lowell the upstart who stole the imagist movement from Pound; Lowell the carnival barker urging people into the New Poetry Show—undoubtedly contain some truth. They by no means reveal the whole person or her achievement.

In the chapters that follow, I review Lowell's life and her critical prose; and then, after considering her first two books, I discuss her monologues and narratives (or what she identified as such) separately from her lyrics. To group together poems with a similar theme, or poems that show variations of a genre, seemed more helpful than following a strict chronological order. Not all of the best of Lowell is here—I had to omit discussion of such fine poems as "Evelyn Ray" and "The Red Knight"; and in fact much more needs to be done with Lowell than can be compassed in a critical introduction to her. But I hope there is enough here to show that she was, besides being an often erratic and uneven writer and a sometimes presumptuous and bossy woman, one of the most important figures of her time and a poet to be reckoned with.

Richard Benvenuto

Michigan State University

Acknowledgments

I thank Houghton Mifflin Company for permission to quote from *The Complete Poetical Works of Amy Lowell,* © 1955 by Houghton Mifflin Company and reprinted by permission of Houghton Mifflin Company; from *Six French Poets* by Amy Lowell, copyright 1915 by Amy Lowell; and from *Amy Lowell: A Chronicle,* by S. Foster Damon, copyright 1935 by S. Foster Damon (© renewed 1963 by S. Foster Damon), reprinted by permission of Houghton Mifflin Company.

G. d'Andelot Belin and Brinton P. Roberts, as trustees under the will of Amy Lowell, have allowed me to quote from the preface to *Some Imagist Poets* (1915) and from the preface to *Some Imagist Poets, 1916;* from Lowell's *Tendencies in Modern American Poetry;* and from Lowell's periodical essays.

I also thank the trustees under the will of Amy Lowell and *Poetry* magazine for allowing me to quote from Amy Lowell's "Eleonora Duse" and from a Lowell letter to Eunice Tietjens, both of which first appeared in *Poetry,* copyright 1923, and reprinted by permission of the editor of *Poetry.*

Poetry has also allowed me to quote from Ezra Pound's "A Few Don'ts from an Imagiste," which first appeared in *Poetry,* copyright 1913, and reprinted by permission of the editor of *Poetry.* I wish to thank New Directions for permission to quote from Ezra Pound, *Selected Letters of Ezra Pound,* copyright 1950 by Ezra Pound and reprinted by permission of New Directions Publishing Corporation. "Oread," from H. D., *Collected Poems: 1912–1944,* © 1982 by the Estate of Hilda Doolittle, is also reprinted by permission of New Directions Publishing Corporation. Permission to quote from Jean Starr Untermeyer, *Private Collection,* © 1965, has been kindly given by Alfred A. Knopf, Inc.

Material from two unpublished letters in the Amy Lowell Collection at Harvard is quoted by permission of the Houghton Library, and G. d'Andelot Belin and Brinton P. Roberts as trustees under the will of Amy Lowell.

I also want to thank Melanie Wisner of the Houghton Reading Room at Harvard University for her prompt and valuable assistance on more than one occasion.

As always, my wife, Joyce, with her quick reflex against humbug, has been my most important sparring partner.

Chronology

1874   Amy Lowell born 9 February in Brookline, Massachusetts.

1883   Lowell begins private school.

1887   *Dream Drops; or, Stories from Fairy Land, by a Dreamer.*

1891   End of formal schooling. Lowell "comes out" and has sixty dinners given in her honor.

1895   Mother dies.

1898   A journey up the Nile does not result in the hoped-for loss of weight; Lowell suffers a prolonged nervous collapse.

1900   Father dies. Lowell acquires Sevenels.

1901   Buys a summer home in New Hampshire. Becomes involved in Brookline community affairs, and makes first public speech.

1902   October, a performance by Eleonora Duse inspires Lowell to become a poet.

1905   Starts her Keats collection.

1910   August, first serious poem, "Fixed Idea."

1912   March, meets Ada Dwyer Russell. September, first issue of *Poetry.* October, *A Dome of Many-Coloured Glass.*

1913   January, reads H. D. and discovers imagism. Meets Harriet Monroe in Chicago. In London for the summer and meets Pound, the other imagists, and John Gould Fletcher. Asked to contribute to *Des Imagistes.*

1914   February, *Des Imagistes.* April, publishes first polyphonic prose poem, "The Forsaken." Summer, quarrels with Pound in London and decides to publish a new imagist anthology—effectively taking over the movement in America. September, *Sword Blades and Poppy Seed.*

1915   March, first public debate over the New Poetry—numerous public readings and lecture tours follow in succeeding years. April, *Some Imagist Poets* (the new anthology). Writes "Patterns." November, *Six French Poets.*

1916   May, *Some Imagist Poets, 1916.* Summer, strains abdominal muscles, eventually leading to hernia. October, *Men, Women and Ghosts.*

1917   April, *Some Imagist Poets, 1917.* Participates in experiments to determine the rhythmic principles of free verse. October, *Tendencies in Modern American Poetry.* Begins working on Chinese poetry with Florence Ayscough.

1918   March, suffers an abdominal rupture. September, first operation for hernia, and *Can Grande's Castle.*

1919   March, becomes the first woman to deliver a lecture at Harvard. September, *Pictures of the Floating World.* November, a fiery argument in Philadelphia over Whitman.

1920   Two more operations for hernia. Receives an honorary degree from Baylor University.

1921   Fourth operation for hernia. Gives Keats Centenary lecture at Yale and decides to write a book on Keats. May, *Legends.* December, *Fir-Flower Tablets.*

1922   Reads her poetry on the radio. September, *A Critical Fable.*

1923   Exhausted and ill after an extended reading tour. December, Eleonora Duse visits Sevenels.

1924   Wins the Helen Haire Levinson prize from *Poetry.*

1925   February, *John Keats.* April, attends a "Complimentary Dinner" in her honor. Suffers a severe hernial attack. Amy Lowell dies on 12 May. August, *What's O'Clock.*

1926   August, *East Wind. What's O'Clock* awarded the Pulitzer Prize.

1927   September, *Ballads for Sale.*

1930   *Poetry and Poets.*

1955   *The Complete Poetical Works of Amy Lowell.*

Chapter One

The Life of Amy Lowell

The most noticeable fact about Amy Lowell's life is its division into two distinct and unequal phases. Until her late thirties, she did little to set her apart from other well-to-do, respectable Boston women. She endured but did not enjoy school; she traveled frequently—to Europe, Egypt, the American West; and she involved herself in local community affairs. Not exactly idle and not ever entirely predictable, until 1912 she was essentially searching for a purpose, for work that would reveal and make use of her talents and help her escape an overactive self-consciousness. These were lonely, sometimes happy, but mostly frustrating years. From 1912 until her death in 1925, Lowell's life was filled with activity—publications, lecture tours, controversies, and feuds. In a matter of months, she made herself a central figure in the literary renaissance that was changing the future of poetry in America—a position she maintained as much by her strength of will as by her talents. She had found a purpose. "Poetry is at once my trade and my religion," she said.[1] She was both a skillful businesswoman and an ardent believer in its cause. More than anyone else, Lowell "put the 'new poetry' 'on the map,' " Elizabeth Sergeant wrote in 1927, "and restored the profession of poet to respectability." Elizabeth Sergeant was one of Lowell's many friends; there were enemies too. But no one who wrote of Lowell—and she was one of the most discussed writers of her time—denied her energy and impact. Most would agree with Sergeant that Lowell "accomplished ten times as much in the last fifteen years of her life as the rest of us in half a century."[2]

Lowell could do as much as she did because she overcame some formidable obstacles: the tradition in the Lowell family that its women not speak in public; her wealth, which she felt caused some editors to treat her unfairly; and most important, her appearance. Lowell was obese; little more than five feet tall, she weighed 240 pounds. Sensitive about her size, Lowell always rode to an appointment, no matter how near, and always covered the mirrors in her hotel rooms. Yet she could make others forget about her size. "One noticed," Louis Untermeyer says, "only the marvelous neatness, the fine hands and delicate ankles, the small mobile mouth, the coolly modulated voice, the quick-appraising but not unkind eyes, the fine features and almost transparent skin. One saw a woman who was not only intelligent but—there is no other word for it—pretty."[3] Some of those less friendly to her called her the hippopoetess. But Lowell could escape her size in narrative poems of other times and places, and in dramatic lyrics she could express loneliness and longings which she, as a fat woman, knew keenly, and that all have felt. Though she always avoided eating in restaurants, because of her self-consciousness about her weight, she read poems very successfully in public and loved large crowds at her readings.

Lowell believed that poets did not choose their subjects; the subjects chose the poets. In a similar way, poetry chose her. She became conscious of her need to be a poet, as a poet becomes aware of the poem in his subconsciousness. The earlier years were a time of evolution to the sudden call of her art. When Lowell was sure she was called to poetry, she responded with all of her considerable might.

Early, Middle, and Restless Years

Amy Lowell was born on 9 February 1874 in Brookline, Massachusetts, then a rural suburb of Boston. She was the youngest of five living children of Augustus and Katherine Lawrence Lowell, who named their home "Sevenels," because it contained seven Lowells. Amy Lowell's room, which she kept all her life and called "Sky Parlour," was on the top floor and overlooked beautiful, patterned gardens, carefully cultivated by her father. Descendants of Percival Lowle, who settled in America in 1639, the Lowells were one of the most prominent and respected families in New England. In the early nineteenth century, they had made a considerable fortune in the cotton industry, as had the Lawrences, Lowell's mother's family. Though in later life Lowell would refute the notion that she was independently wealthy, and though she always tried to get as much money for her poems and public readings as she could, she was in fact rich and never had to work to support herself. Ferris Greenslet, her close friend and editor at Houghton Mifflin, estimated that at the time of her father's death in 1900, Lowell's income "ran close to six figures."[4]

Successful in business, the Lowells also strongly supported education and the arts. Amy Lowell's great-grandfather was one of the founders of the Boston Athenaeum, the library that Lowell felt contributed more to her learning than any school. Her grandfather was the first trustee of the Lowell Institute, which had been founded by his cousin. Another cousin of his was the poet James Russell Lowell. Four generations of Lowells served as fellows of Harvard College, and Lowell's father was an officer in various learned societies. Percival Lowell, her oldest brother, wrote several books about the Far East before he became a noted astronomer; her other brother, Lawrence, became president of Harvard. Literary interests were strong at Sevenels, which had a well-stocked library even before Lowell began her extensive collection. The first book Lowell ever wanted to own—she kept it all of her life—was *Rollo Learning to Read,* which many years before her grandmother had given to her mother. "The mere touch of that straight-grained morocco was a delight," Lowell recalled; "the old wood cuts, colored with crayons doubtless by my mother, were to me gems of the purest art. Could I read at that date? I doubt it. But I demanded the stories again and again; I verily believe I could repeat them by heart now."[5] Another moment of her early childhood that stood out for her years later was a dinner party at which she was carried around the table in a scrap basket by Henry Wadsworth Longfellow.[6]

Lowell was proud of her heritage, of being a Lowell. Her longtime friend Elizabeth Ward Perkins speaks of Lowell's "intense loyalty" to her family. "The family was never forgotten or neglected; clan connections and interests were close."[7] Certainly Lowell had the energy, industry, and strong will of her forebears. Yet her family does not seem to loom large in her personal life and still less in her public career. Percival, whom she probably esteemed and liked the best of her family, was nearly nineteen years old when Lowell was born; Lawrence was seventeen. Her two sisters, Katherine and Elizabeth, were sixteen and twelve. Her parents were middle-aged, and her mother suffered from Bright's disease. Thus, almost a whole generation separated Lowell from the youngest members of her immediate family, and two generations stood between her and her parents. Raising her was delegated to her sister Elizabeth, who says that Lowell was both neglected and spoiled by her parents: "Parents who have devoted much time and energy for many years to bringing up a family are tired and want to rest, and so a belated child is not apt to be disciplined except when he or she annoys the weary parent. This was very much the case with Amy, and she was never taught self-control un-

less it affected their personal comfort."[8] Elizabeth Ward Perkins remembers both the lively dinner parties at Sevenels when Lowell's
brothers and sisters were present, talking and listening simultaneously, and the changed, formal atmosphere when she and Lowell were
alone with the parents: "The mother's invalidism, and the father's
stern conventions as to time and order, even in the conventional
nineties, left non-conformist youth without sun or sun-warmed air to
breathe."[9]

But the stern conventions and settled habits of her parents did not
darken Lowell's childhood. She was a tomboy who loved to roam the
nine-and-a-half acres of land around her home, shooting imaginary
Indians and pretending to be Robin Hood or the Last of the Mohi-
cans. She also spent much of her time in the Sevenels stables, fascinated by horses and the stories of the man who took care of them, an
ex-jockey named Burns. She learned to handle horses well and, when
she was older, enjoyed driving her own horse and carriage at fast
speeds. At about six years old, she was sent to Papanti's dancing
school in Boston, to prepare her for her formal "coming out" as a
young woman. But she identified more with boyish activities, and
according to her childhood friend Katie Dana, Lowell "deeply grieved
that she was not a boy. She always tried to walk exactly like her
brothers Percy and Lawrence, striding along with her head down and
her hat crammed over her ears." When asked, "What is your idea of
misery," Lowell responded, "Not to be allowed to tobbogan."[10]

An English governess began teaching Lowell to read and write
when she was five or six; at eight, she was sent to school. By then
she had developed a strong love of reading and had even begun some
juvenile writings. The first Rollo book had whetted her appetite for
the whole collection. She brought friends home and read the Rollo
books out loud to them, an activity she always enjoyed and in which
she would eventually excel. She loved fairy stories—Hans Christian
Andersen; adventure and sea stories—Cooper and Marryat; and went
on to Dickens, Thackeray, and the major Victorian novelists. She
read all of Scott, and near the end of her life could remember vividly
going as a young girl with her brother to a secondhand book store to
buy a complete set of Scott. It was the first major purchase of her
extensive book collection. Lowell was, in her own words, "an omni-
vorous reader," and like many who have a passion for books, she felt
an early urge to write. In 1882 she started a "Private Book," containing her first character sketches; "Amy's Journal," of the same

year, was a record of events during a whirlwind tour of Europe with her parents and sisters. In 1883 she wrote a poem, "Chacago" *(sic),* while returning from a trip to California. With Katie Dana, she brought out one issue of a "Sevenels Gazette." In 1887 Lowell dictated a number of stories to her mother, some of them her own, some learned from members of the family. The collection, published as *Dream Drops; or, Stories from Fairy Land, by a Dreamer,* was sold at a fair to raise money for the Perkins Institution, which that year had sent a teacher to Helen Keller. One of Lowell's original contributions, "What Made Willy Bright Like to Go to Bed," shows genuine narrative skill, and is a very readable children's story.[11] "My imagination was a very obtrusive factor in my life," Lowell says of these years, "and was not, happily, left without food."[12]

Her imaginative life no doubt compensated her for the lack of peer companionship at home, and provided a refuge from the growing awareness of her awkwardness and from a lonely self-consciousness that would eventually lead to nervous collapse. Her obesity—apparently glandular in origin, though Lowell did enjoy big meals—had begun to manifest itself by the time she was eight. As she approached adolescence, her stoutness humiliated her. In her diary for 1889, she exhibits signs of despondency and self-hate. "If I were not so self-conscious I would be much better. Everybody thinks I'm a fool (& it's true) & nobody cares a hang about me." Her more attractive schoolmates and friends were becoming interested in boys, and suddenly Lowell discovered that she was in love with a Paul H. She takes a brutally honest view of her chances of attracting him:

It is so silly; but when Paul asks Mabel to walk with him I feel just like going off alone somewhere & crying. This feeling is mixed by a kind of wish to hit Somebody.

If there was any chance of Paul's ever loving me it would be different & I should not be ready to pound myself for being such a fool as to love him.

But I am ugly, fat, conspicuous, & dull; to say nothing of a very bad temper.

She is sure she will be an old maid: "nobody could love me I know. Why, if I were somebody-els, I should hate my-self."[13]

With her brothers and sisters all married or gone from the house by the time she was twelve, and her mother increasingly ill, Lowell was lonely. She longed for one close friend, "a *very* intimate friend, a friend whom I should love better than any other girl in the world,

& who would feel so towards me. To whom I could tell all that is in
my heart & who would do so towards me."[14] Years later, she wrote
of "the loneliness of surrounding, from which all the poets of this
generation have suffered."[15] The various schools she attended had little to offer that she valued, and Lowell was not a good student. She
could not—at least did not—apply herself, and she was undisciplined
in class. She felt that she stood out from the other students because
of her size; she could not abide the rote, mechanical learning that she
felt the curriculum consisted of. When she left school for good at seventeen, she judged her formal education as not amounting to "a hill
of beans," and carried with her a lifelong negative view of education
in America.[16]

But despite her blue periods, Lowell had a strong zest for life. She
made her formal coming out in the fall of 1891, attending sixty dinners given in her honor that year, and was a popular debutante who
loved to dance. Although her writing seems to have stopped, she continued and expanded her reading. She enjoyed the theater. Entranced
by a performance of Victor Hugo's *Ruy Blas,* in May 1894 she began
in earnest the study of French, which she had neglected in school, in
order to read Hugo in the original. Hugo, Lowell says, woke her up
"to the meaning of style. I was lifted on the wings of a great poetry,
although so little had poetry been a thing which I considered, I did
not know it was that."[17] She taught herself so well that she knew
French better than any of her colleagues in the imagist group except
F. S. Flint, and Flint said that she read French beautifully.[18]

On 1 April 1895, when Lowell was twenty-one, her mother died
of Bright's disease—an end that was not unexpected and probably
brought a sense of release. Lowell visited Europe with friends in
1896, and in 1897 became romantically involved with a young Bostonian who apparently proposed marriage to her. According to Foster
Damon, "the engagement was all but announced" when the man became "entangled elsewhere" and broke off the relationship.[19] Possibly
blaming her obesity for her lover's desertion, determining in any
event to do something about it, Lowell spent the winter of 1897–98
in Egypt, where she made a three-month trip up the Nile in the hope
that heat and a severely restricted diet would reduce her weight.
Egypt fascinated her and expanded her cultural horizons, but the experiment left her exhausted, just as fat as before, and in the grip of
a nervous prostration from which she did not fully recover for seven
years. When her father died in 1900, she had already taken two more

journeys, to California and England, in an attempt to recover from the effects of the trip to Egypt.

After her father's death, Lowell was mistress of Sevenels, but she was far from well, and at twenty-six had accomplished nothing of note and had no prospect of a career. She spent the next decade involving herself in community affairs. She led a group that successfully opposed the moving of the Boston Athenaeum to a new site, and she was the first Lowell woman to speak in public, when she argued, again successfully, for the dismissal of an incapacitated school official. She traveled, bought a summer home in New Hampshire, and when her health improved, remodeled Sevenels and began to entertain extensively. She especially enjoyed theatrical and musical performances at her home, and participated herself in amateur theatrical productions in Boston. The theater might well have been her chosen career, if she had not been so overweight. She met the musician Carl Engel, who introduced her to the work of the most modern and, at the time, controversial, composers. In 1909, her stables and horses were destroyed by fire, and the next year Lowell began to raise large sheepdogs, which were to become a terror to more than one of her guests. The years between 1900 and 1910, that is, were largely filled with the activities and interests of a prominent, well-to-do, but otherwise unexceptional woman. But because of a book she had read sometime in the past and a performance she attended in 1902, these were also the years in which Lowell began to write poetry seriously.

Finding a Vocation: A Poet Born and Reborn

The date is uncertain, but shortly after Lowell left school she discovered Leigh Hunt's *Imagination and Fancy: or, Selections from the English Poets,* the book that, she said, "opened a door" for her "that might otherwise have remained shut." She found the book in her father's library and was attracted to it instantly. "I did not read it, I devoured it. I read it over and over, and then I turned to the works of the poets referred to, and tried to read them by the light of the new aesthetic perception I had learned from Hunt." Just as she had done with the Rollo books, she "inveigled" friends to her room to read them Hunt's selections from Shelley, Keats, Coleridge, and Beaumont and Fletcher.[20] Hunt's book, designed to teach the general reader how to identify poetry of the highest quality, consists of a long essay entitled "What is Poetry," and separate chapters on major Renaissance and romantic poets. Hunt quotes extensively from each (including the whole of "The Eve of St. Agnes"), and underscores the best or most imaginative lines. His style is similar to Lowell's own later prose—direct, informal, conversational; it was almost certainly an influence on her. Hunt speaks of the importance of music in poetry, as opposed to strict or mechanical meter, arguing that the number of syllables in a line or phrase can and should vary as much as the number of notes in a bar of music. To consider the music of poetry simply in terms of "feet and syllables . . . iambics or trochees" is to reduce it "to less than its dry bones."[21] Lowell argued the same point in numerous essays the last ten years of her life. The academic criticism of her schools had irritated Lowell. Hunt taught her to enjoy poetry, to value it as an art, and to recognize the skills that make it beautiful. And he began her lifelong love of Keats.

In October 1902 the great Italian actress Eleonora Duse performed in Boston. Lowell had almost certainly seen her during earlier American tours in the 1890s, but the 1902 performance stirred her deeply. Returning home, she wrote a poem to express her feelings—and twenty-one years later published it in *Poetry* magazine, as part of a special issue containing juvenile poems by established poets. She sent the following letter with the poem:

I have had rather a curious writing life. I used to write poems as a little girl, but I was no Hilda Conkling—they were ordinary verse of little girls, and of no value whatever. From the time I was about fifteen or sixteen I had a pause, I wrote nothing till I was twenty-eight, which is sufficiently strange, I think. Then I suddenly burst into poetry, and I have never ceased since. . . . Eleonora Duse came to America on one of her periodical trips; that was the year she was acting in the d'Annunzio plays. I went to see her, as I always went to see everything that was good in the theatre. The effect on me was tremendous. What really happened was that it revealed me to myself, but I hardly knew it at the time. I just knew that I had got to express the sensations that Duse's acting gave me, somehow. I knew nothing whatever of the technique of poetry, I had never heard of *vers libre*. I had never analyzed blank verse—I was as ignorant as anyone could be. I sat down, and with infinite agitation wrote this poem. It has, I think, every *cliché* and every technical error which a poem can have, but it loosed a bolt in my brain and I found out where my true function lay.[22]

The poem, "Eleonora Duse," is seventy-one lines long, mostly in blank verse. Although it is flawed, it is not nearly as bad as Lowell says it is, especially considering that it is her first serious effort to write poetry. Duse's presence and impact are strongly expressed:

> For she whom we have come to see tonight
> Is more to be divined and felt than seen,
> And when she comes one yields one's heart perforce,
> As one might yield some noble instrument
> For her to draw its latent music forth.[23]

Moved by a powerfully creative woman, Lowell's own creativity awoke.

She did not, of course, decide that night to make poetry her career. Her interests were in the theater, music, remodeling Sevenels. But the first poem led naturally to others, until gradually Lowell was spending more and more time on her writing. In 1910, she made her first attempt to place her work, by sending four sonnets to the *Atlantic Monthly,* which accepted them. "A Fixed Idea," her first published poem, appeared in the *Atlantic* in August 1910. By 1912 she had completed the manuscript of her first book, *A Dome of Many-Coloured Glass.* Her life would change significantly after 1912—which, by a singular coincidence, was the year that marked a major turning point in American poetry.

Lowell had found her vocation. But just as important to her, she found someone to share it with when she met Ada Dwyer (Mrs. Harold Russell) at an informal luncheon on 12 March 1912.[24] Eleven years older than Lowell, Ada Dwyer was a professional actress and was performing in Boston that February and March. She was also, Lowell quickly decided, perfectly suited to be the "very intimate friend" Lowell had wanted since childhood. Attractive, sensitive, well-educated, Dwyer had an intelligent interest in poetry and was a good listener. Lowell had a strong interest in the theater, Dwyer's professional sphere. Lowell invited her new friend to Sevenels, where she read her the poems in *A Dome of Many-Coloured Glass;* Dwyer promised to visit her that summer in New Hampshire, and soon Lowell was urging her to give up acting entirely and make Sevenels her permanent home, which Dwyer agreed to do early in 1914. The effect on Lowell of Dwyer's companionship can only be estimated, but it was unquestionably important and beneficial. Lowell found it difficult and painful to part with her, when Dwyer visited relatives in Utah (she was separated from her husband) or her daughter in Washington,

D.C. Lowell's great creative output between 1914 and 1925 would
not have been possible without her friend's steadying, supportive
presence. Dwyer became indispensable to the smooth running of daily
affairs at Sevenels. As her career took form, Lowell followed a special
and demanding schedule. She wrote all night while the rest of the
house slept; went to bed at dawn, when the others were getting up;
breakfasted in the middle of the afternoon; and entertained her
friends in the evening until midnight, the start of her working day.
It was Ada Dwyer who kept the house quiet, yet busy, while Lowell
slept, who went to the library for books Lowell needed, and who entertained guests and presided over dinner until Lowell finally appeared—Lowell was always late for appointments and often arrived at
her own table an hour after her guests had been seated and eating.
Dwyer was a calming influence, which the quick-tempered, argumen-
tative poet needed; and she took away the loneliness that Lowell had
feared since her school days. Some of Lowell's best poems express her
love for Ada Dwyer; she thought of her work as a whole as belonging
to both of them, and once suggested that they have a sign made with
their two names on it as "Makers of Fine Poems."[25]

At about the time Lowell first met Ada Dwyer, Carl Engel introduced her to the work of the French symbolists and their successors.
Most of her reading in poetry had been from the authors covered by
Leigh Hunt and the traditional American and British Victorians:
Lowell and Longfellow, Browning and Arnold. The poems in *A Dome
of Many-Coloured Glass* reflect her readings and follow the accepted
conventions of meter, stanza form, and rhyme. Now, as she was
about to take her manuscript to a publisher, Lowell discovered free
verse—which she preferred to call cadenced verse or *vers libre*—and
a much more modern kind of poetry than her own. While her manuscript was being read, she wrote her first free-verse poem, "Before
the Altar," to replace the more conventional "Apples of Hesperides"
as the first poem in the book. *A Dome of Many-Coloured Glass* appeared on 12 October 1912. Like all of her subsequent books of poetry, its format, at Lowell's request, was "modelled as closely as
possible on the first edition of Keats's *Lamia*."[26]

Lowell's first book received lukewarm reviews at best, but its publication put her into direct touch with the poetic world at the most
appropriate time for her career. Deep and vital changes were reshap-
ing poetry. Almost simultaneously with the *Dome*, Ezra Pound's *Ri-*

postes appeared in London, with an appendix containing "the complete
poetical works"—five poems—of T. E. Hulme, the founder of imagism. It made the first mention in print of imagism. Pound had already taken over the imagist movement, was agitating for its
acceptance, had met F. S. Flint and discovered H. D. (Hilda Doolittle) and her future husband, Richard Aldington. In that same October Robert Frost's first book, *A Boy's Will,* was accepted in London;
and in Chicago, the first issue of Harriet Monroe's *Poetry* magazine
appeared, which soon became a major source of support for younger
poets. The New Poetry movement had begun. "New Books of Poetry
were popping like Popcorn," Vachel Lindsay recalled; "and all the
poets in America for the first time in thirty years were looking one
another in the eye."[27]

Lowell was eager to become part of what seemed to many an elec-
triclike poetic renaissance. She learned of the forthcoming issue of
Poetry in September 1912—Monroe had seen her poems in the *Atlantic*—sent twenty-five dollars to support the magazine, and later sub-
mitted some poems. She met Harriet Monroe in Chicago early in
1913—the beginning of a long, warm, and sometimes stormy relationship. With Ezra Pound as its foreign correspondent, *Poetry* introduced Lowell to imagism and determined her to investigate it. The
January 1913 issue contained poems by Hilda Doolittle that were
signed "H. D., 'Imagiste.' " As Lowell read the poems, it "suddenly . . . came over her: 'Why, I, too, am an Imagiste!' "[28] But she
could hardly have known what she was saying, knowing practically
nothing about imagism, and writing a very different kind of poetry
from H. D.'s. In March, *Poetry* printed an article, signed by Flint,
explaining the principles of imagism, and followed it with Pound's
"A Few Don'ts by an Imagiste." The imagists called for precision,
economy, definiteness, and direct treatment; they warned against ab-
stractions, rhetoric, and dead-stop iambic lines. Pound stressed the
poet's need to learn from the musician, not only about flexible
rhythm or cadence as opposed to mechanical meter, but also about
the discipline necessary to his craft: "Don't imagine that the art of
poetry is any simpler than the art of music, or that you can please
the expert before you have spent at least as much effort on the art of
verse as the average piano teacher spends on the art of music."[29]

Her interest aroused by these and other discussions of modern poetry in the early issues of *Poetry,* Lowell decided to find out more

about imagism, firsthand, from Pound himself. With a letter of introduction from Harriet Monroe, she went to London to meet Pound in the summer of 1913.

It was a productive trip for her. Pound, impressed with Lowell as "both generous and genuinely interested in modern poetry," took pains to acquaint her with imagist ideas and practice. He introduced her to Hulme's theories, discussed recent French uses of vers libre, and read his poems to her. "I think I see more clearly what imagism really is," Lowell said. "I don't suppose I have written a single poem that could possibly fit your definition, but I would like to try it."[30] Stimulated that summer as she "had never been before," she wrote "The Precinct, Rochester," "White and Green," "Aubade," "The Captured Goddess," "A London Thoroughfare, 2 a.m.," and other poems that appeared in *Sword Blades and Poppy Seed,* her second book. She read her latest poems to John Gould Fletcher, who was becoming a firm friend, and who thought that she had copied some of his techniques—detailed observation rather than generalization, and the use of "orchestral color words."[31] Fletcher was probably right, but the larger truth is that Lowell was developing rapidly as a poet, learning as much as she could from anyone in order to catch up with the new poetry. At thirty-nine, she was more than ten years older than most of her new acquaintances—Pound was twenty-eight, and Fletcher, twenty-seven. But she had as much vitality and intellectual curiosity as they, and much more promotional know-how. She was largely responsible for the publication of Fletcher's *Irradiations,* which he read to her that summer.

Shortly after her return home, she agreed to Pound's request to include her poem "In a Garden" in an anthology he was planning. In 1914, her poems began to appear in increasing numbers in the journals—five in the February *Egoist,* eight in the April *Poetry*—and she was already becoming a prolific writer of essays and reviews. Pound's anthology *Des Imagistes* had appeared in the February issue of the *Glebe,* a relatively obscure monthly; it was published in book form in April. The anthology contains no preface or introduction; no one is named as editor; and no reason is given for grouping the poets it contains (they included, among others, James Joyce, William Carlos Williams, and Allen Upward). It was widely but, Lowell thought, ignorantly reviewed. By May, the proofs of *Sword Blades and Poppy Seed* had been corrected, Ada Dwyer had become her permanent companion, and having thought of how to advance the imagist cause and present it more favorably to the public, Lowell again went to England for the summer. It was to be her last trip abroad. She arrived in early July 1914. While she was on the Atlantic, the archduke of Austria was assassinated. No one anticipated the terrible global conflict just ahead; nor did Lowell foresee the personal battle that waited for her.

The Quarrel with Pound

Lowell and Pound had responded warmly to each other in 1913. Pound taught Lowell a great deal, introduced her to some of the important younger and established writers in London, and, in effect, initiated her into the imagist movement. In February 1914, he invited her to edit the *Egoist,* urging her to purchase the journal and consider living half the year in London. His intelligence, high standards, and devotion to poetry had very favorably impressed Lowell. "What especially pleases me," she wrote Harriet Monroe, from England in 1913, "is his evident interest in my work. Mr. Pound is no flatterer, but his reticent praise is good to hear, and his occasional criticisms are very much to the point. He is reading me the Ms. of his new book some day this week." She was struck by "his personal charm . . . and youthful enthusiasm which keeps him talking delightfully as many hours as you please; the violence of his writings giving way to show a very thin-skinned and sensitive personality opening out like a flower in a sympathetic circle, and I should imagine shutting up like a clam in an alien atmosphere." She feels sure that he will outgrow some of his theories and not confine himself to any school. "He is so young that all sorts of developments may be expected." Thanking Monroe for her letter of introduction to Pound, Lowell felt that she had made, not only "a personal friend, but, through his kindness, a little wedge into the heart of English letters."[32] She most certainly was looking forward to meeting Pound again.

But Pound, true to Lowell's prediction, was going beyond the confines of his own school. Without exactly abandoning imagism, he had organized another movement, vorticism, more radical than imagism and more concerned with connections among all the arts. It had its own periodical, as strident and aggressive as its name, *BLAST,* of which only two issues were published. Not very interested in vorticism, Lowell wanted to discuss the future of imagism and the possibilities of a better organized imagist anthology. She attended, at Pound's invitation, a vorticist dinner, but felt out of place. Two nights later, on 17 July, she gave her own dinner party to celebrate, belatedly, the *Des Imagistes* anthology. The scene was being set for a contest between two domineering, quick-tempered personalities over the leadership of the new poetry. Pound had every right to consider himself the head of the imagist school, but he now seemed, to Lowell, to be involved in different interests. And the year since she had first met him had brought important changes to Lowell. She had "become transformed," Fletcher says, "from the obscure amateur of *A Dome of Many-Coloured Glass* to the professional leader of the new poets. From being a mere student and a pupil of her younger contemporaries, she was already on her way towards becoming their most picturesquely popular defender. . . . She had already grown so important as to be able now successfully to dispute the leadership of the group with Ezra Pound."³³ Fletcher somewhat overstates Lowell's position in July 1914, but not what she was soon to become.

Lowell's imagist dinner, still a memorable evening to Fletcher when he described it twenty-three years later, was a bizarre affair. Lowell called upon Ford Madox Hueffer, who was later to revile her, to make a speech. Hueffer said that he did not know what an imagist poet was, but doubted whether Lowell or even Pound could be called one. Allen Upward, the next speaker, also said that he did not know what an imagist poet was, but that Amy Lowell might be considered an imagist if "Ezra found it in his heart to say so publicly." Richard Aldington restricted imagism to the restoration of the Hellenic view of life. While he was arguing this point with the sculptor Gaudier-Brzeska, Pound slipped out through the waiter's entrance, returning in a few minutes with a large tin bathtub on his head. This, Pound said, should be the symbol of a new school, not imagist, but "nageiste," named after the concluding lines of Lowell's poem, "In a Garden": "Night, and the water, and you in your whiteness, bathing!" Lowell joined in the laughter, though it was at her expense. In fact, she comported herself well throughout the evening, with a dignity and a grace that must have struck others there as more promising in a leader than the antics of Pound.³⁴

But it was Pound's dictatorial ways—or what they felt to be such—that drove some of the imagists to what was becoming the Lowell camp. That spring, before coming to England, Lowell had written, with Pound's blessing, a poem foreboding their conflict: "Astigmatism: To Ezra Pound, With Much Friendship and Admiration and Some Differences of Opinion." It describes a poet who kills all flowers that are not roses, leaving one beautiful field after another in waste, because only roses satisfy him. If this was less than fair to Pound, it was not a view of him confined only to Lowell. She persuaded Aldington, H. D., and Flint that the next imagist anthology should be more democratically managed than *Des Imagistes* had been, with the poets equally represented in terms of space, and no one given more authority than the others in judging what was fit to be included. She had no thought of excluding Pound—he had given "Imagisme," in the French spelling by which it was still known, its name. Pound, however, would not cooperate. He wanted "Imagisme" to keep "some sort of meaning," he said, and to have a definite standard as a poetry of "light, clear edges." He could not trust "a dam'd contentious, probably incompetent" and "democratized committee to maintain that standard. Some will be splay-footed and some sentimental." He did promise not to stand in Lowell's way or try to dissuade anyone from joining her—generously, he said he would not publish an anthology of his own in America before 1916. He did want it known that he dissociated himself from Lowell's anthology, and he objected to the use of "Imagisme" in the title. He wrote Lowell, "If you want to drag in the word Imagisme you can use a subtitle 'an anthology devoted to Imagisme, vers libre and modern movements in verse' or something of that sort. I think that will be perfectly fair to everyone."[35]

Pound was trying to be fair; he also wanted to have the last word on what imagism was. Lowell, much less concerned with dogmatic principles or schools, hoped to make the new poetry known to a wider audience than it had reached so far. She undertook, Aldington says, "to do all the practical work, to get the books published in Boston and London, and to account to us for the royalties. And well and loyally she discharged that task, which involved a good deal of work and correspondence."[36] She was scrupulously honest about the royalties of the three anthologies that resulted from her efforts, dividing the money into six shares for herself and her five associates. Besides Aldington, H. D., and Flint—who had been with her in Pound's anthology—she persuaded Fletcher to join. And to replace Pound, she obtained a writer she met that summer whom she thought far more promising, D. H. Lawrence. Her friendship with Lawrence, involving many letters between them, lasted the rest of her life.

The outbreak of the war delayed Lowell's return home. She spent most of August working with a committee set up by Herbert Hoover to help Americans fleeing the Continent, often without their money or baggage. She got back to America in time for the publication of *Sword Blades and Poppy Seed* in September—the book that Damon says "really began" her career, and which was much more favorably received than the *Dome*. She now had very different feelings about Pound from the year before. It was no longer a mere quarrel between them, she wrote to Harriet Monroe on 15 September, it was a "schism." Pound was angry with her for refusing to give five thousand dollars to a journal of which he hoped to be made editor. She thought she could do more for poets "less fortunate" than herself by financing a yearly imagist anthology. Pound "sent for the Aldingtons and told them they must choose between him and me, which was awful for them, as he is a very old friend, and has done much for them, and I was only a new friend. . . . They told Ezra it was not a question of me at all, but a question of principle, that they felt it only fair to let the poets choose their own contributions and to give each poet equal space. He then tried to bribe them, by asking them to get up an Anthology with him, and leave me out. This they absolutely refused to do." The attempted bribe helps to explain why Lowell no longer saw Pound as "a youthful phenomenon," but rather as "falling back at every step, and this naturally makes him exceedingly bitter. He is very brilliant, but he does not work enough, and his work lacks the quality of soul, which, I am more and more fain to believe, no great work can ever be without."[37]

Lowell told Monroe that the new anthology would be called "Some Imagiste Poets." Pound objected so strongly to the use of "Imagiste" that the Macmillan Company, which was considering publication, returned the manuscript to Lowell, who then took it to Houghton Mifflin. Pound felt that much of his work would be undone if he allowed Lowell—a rank newcomer, in his eyes—to turn imagism into "a democratic beer-garden." He, too, complained to Harriet Monroe. "A. L. comes over here, gets kudos out of association. She returns and wants to weaken the whole use of the term imagist, by making it mean *any* writing of vers libre. Why, if they want to be vers-librists, why can't they say so? But no, she wants in Lawrence, Fletcher, her own looser work. And the very discrimination, the whole core of significance I've taken twelve years of discipline to get at, she expects me to accord to people who have taken fifteen minutes' survey of my results."[38] What especially infuriated Pound was the advertisement for Lowell's *Sword Blades and Poppy Seed,* in which she was called the "foremost member of the 'Imagists'—a group of poets that includes

William Butler Yeats, Ezra Pound, Ford Madox Hueffer."[39] To add to the annoyance of finding himself placed second to a relative beginner, who did not know what imagism was a short time before, there was the loose use of the term to include two poets—Yeats and Hueffer—who were not imagists. "I think you had better cease referring to yourself as an Imagiste," he wrote Lowell on 19 October 1914, "more especially as *The Dome of Glass* certainly has no aspirations in our direction."[40] He threatened, not very seriously perhaps, to sue her for libel—which she invited him to do, as it would result in new jackets for her book and be good advertising for it. Although she was "exceedingly sorry" for the advertisement and objected to it herself, she did feel that, having been asked by him to be in the first imagist anthology, she had a right to consider herself part of the movement.[41]

There was still the question of the title of the fought-over anthology. No one wanted to alienate Pound; Houghton Mifflin, on the other hand, did not want to drop "Imagiste" from the title. Other suggestions—"The Six," "Some Twentieth Century Poets"—were too indefinite. Finally, it was decided to anglicize "Imagiste" by dropping the final "e." *Some Imagist Poets,* the first of three annual anthologies containing the work of the same six writers, appeared on 17 April 1915. Unlike *Des Imagistes,* it contained a preface, written by Aldington and revised by Lowell, explaining the principal tenets of imagism and the format of the book. Pound is not mentioned or alluded to, although the preface advocates the same kind of poetry he called for in his earlier essay, "A Few Don'ts by an Imagiste." Probably to assert their independence from Pound, the poets in the new anthology disavow membership in any particular school. "We wish it to be clearly understood that we do not represent an exclusive artistic sect; we publish our work together because of mutual artistic sympathy, and we propose to bring out our cooperative volume each year for a short term of years, until we have made a place for ourselves and our principles such as we desire."[42] By explaining their theory of imagism, Lowell expected a modest success for the book. She "never suspected," Damon says, "the thunderstorms of controversy over the Imagist credo that were to recur and reverberate for several years."[43] The anthology and her defense of it made Lowell, in America at least, the leader of imagism.

The quarrel with Pound never ended. In 1917, Pound accused Lowell of wanting him "to sell out lock stock and barrel" for the anthology. "You tried to stampede me into accepting as my artistic equals various people whom it would have been rank hypocrisy for me to accept in any such manner. There is no democracy in the arts."[44] Lowell, an aristocrat, a member of one of Boston's oldest families, did not advocate democracy in the arts—in fact, she agreed with Pound on the point; but she did insist on an equal suffrage for herself and for those whose work she believed in. She was convinced that her poetry and influence were on the rise, Pound's on the decline. She acknowledged Pound's important role at the beginning of the imagist movement, and continued to admire his poetry, but she argued that credit for the success of the movement should go to her, not Pound. She began to think of Pound as a bitter enemy. She refused to support or submit to journals that Pound was involved with. She belittled writers—James Joyce, T. S. Eliot—that Pound boosted; in 1922, she refused to contribute toward a fund that Pound and Aldington were trying to gather for Eliot. Pound, for his part, scornfully referred to her branch of the imagist movement as amygism. It was indeed a schism between the uncompromising, tyrannical expatriot and the ambitious, recognition-hungry Bostonian. They may have had too many traits in common to get along with each other: after telling Pound that imagism could not be copyrighted by him, Lowell considered copyrighting the name herself. Or, as Harriet Monroe explains the quarrel, "two captains, each accustomed to command, could not get on together in the same boat."[45]

In the Thick of the Battle for the New Poetry

It is also true that, until ill health finally wore her out, Lowell thrived on disputes, controversies, and literary quarrels. Pugnacious and strong-willed, she did not shrink from the battle for the new poetry, but took the offensive. Given five minutes to address the Poetry Society of America at its March 1915 meeting, and hoping to create interest in her forthcoming imagist anthology, Lowell precipitated a vocal brawl, the first of many. She read "Bath," a poem she had written in the form she called polyphonic prose. It describes the sensations, mostly of color, experienced by someone in a bathtub:

Little spots of sunshine lie on the surface of the water and dance, dance, and their reflections wobble deliciously over the ceiling; a stir of my finger sets them whirring, reeling. I move a foot, and the planes of light in the water jar. I lie back and laugh, and let the green-white water, the sun-flawed beryl water, flow over me. The day is almost too bright to bear, the green water covers me from the too bright day. I will lie here awhile and play with the water and the sun spots.[46]

She had barely finished, according to Jean Untermeyer, "when she was assailed, and with ill-bred hostility. Questions shot at her from every part of the room; it was almost like a planned bombardment." The conservative wing of the Poetry Society objected to the bathtub as an unfit subject for poetry, and questioned whether the prose lines Lowell read were poetry at all. In the midst of the "bedlam" that was let loose, Jessie Rittenhouse says that Lowell remained calm, an opinion supported by Untermeyer. "Then Amy performed in a manner I have never yet seen equaled by man or woman. The assaults—sometimes in the form of a question, sometimes of an accusation—came at her pell-mell. Amy stood her ground and kept her poise. With unparalleled accuracy she kept tabs on her hecklers and answered them brilliantly, seriatim. I sat in open-mouthed admiration and almost blistered my palms applauding."[47]

Lowell was nowhere more at home than when reading or lecturing before a large audience, and in the years that followed she produced in thousands of listeners the enthusiasm felt by Mrs. Untermeyer. Whether the audience was supportive or hostile did not matter to Lowell, so long as it was responsive. On one occasion, after she had finished reading her first poem, her listeners did not know whether to applaud immediately or wait to the end of the last poem. Lowell confronted them: "Well?—Clap or hiss, I don't care which; but do something!"[48] Enormously successful and in great demand, she traveled extensively on reading-lecture tours—once as far as to Omaha—even when her health was failing. At the height of her fame, people had to be turned away from the auditoriums and halls she used, even though the aisles had been filled, and extra chairs set along the walls to accommodate as many as possible. In 1920, over 1,200 people heard her at the University of Chicago; two years later, she read to 2,500 at the University of Michigan. Frost was in Ann Arbor and introduced her. Before she could begin, her special reading lamp—a high-powered light that she used because of eye trouble—blew out a fuse, plunging the hall in darkness. "The janitor could not be found for half an hour; meanwhile Miss Lowell and Frost kept the invisible audience in howls of laughter by their impromptu jests."[49] Frost, who did not highly regard Lowell's poetry, acknowledged her power over a live audience.

Lowell's reading tours—many and exhausting—helped to make the new poetry a matter of national interest. Of course she appreciated the promotional value for her own work of appearing in the papers as the center of some debate or the performer before capacity crowds—

before 1915, she made headlines because she smoked cigars and was
the sister of the president of Harvard. But she read and promoted the
works of others as well: Carl Sandburg, Fletcher, Lawrence, H. D. In
effect, these and other poets that she liked became almost a family to
her, filling the void left by the generation gap in her own family. She
knew she could do even more for poetry as the poetry editor of a journal. Pound's connection with *Poetry* gave him an advantage over her,
and Lowell disparaged him to Monroe in more than one letter, almost
certainly hoping to replace his influence with her own.[50] Monroe
liked Lowell, but remained faithful to Pound. In January 1915, Lowell went to Chicago to persuade Margaret Anderson into making her
the poetry editor of Anderson's newly formed *Little Review*. "I love
the *Little Review*," Lowell told Anderson, "and I have money. You
haven't. Take me with you. I'll pay you one hundred and fifty dollars
a month, and you'll remain in full control, I'll merely direct your
poetry department. You can count on me never to dictate." Anderson
could not count on that, and refused the offer. "Amy was furious.
She concealed it. She argued, implored. I could see that she had set
her mind on the idea. But she had a redeeming trait—when she was
finally convinced that I meant what I said she dropped the subject
and never reverted to it." Instead, she invited Anderson to lunch the
next day.[51]

One can only guess how Lowell would have found time to be poetry editor of the *Little Review*. Besides her reading tours and numerous essays and reviews, she published nine books, including the huge
biography of Keats, in the last ten years of her life, and left enough
manuscripts for three more after her death. In February 1915, she
began a series of biographical-critical lectures on modern French poetry, which she published as *Six French Poets* the following November.
Shortly after the lectures she wrote "Patterns," which the *Little Review*
published in August 1915. Lowell knew she had written a great
poem and used "Patterns" to open her third book of poetry, *Men,
Women and Ghosts*, published in October 1916. *Men, Women and
Ghosts* contains primarily narrative poetry, but with extensive exper-
imentation and a wide variety of forms: metrical verse, free verse, and
polyphonic prose. *Can Grande's Castle*, published two years later, in
September 1918, was more experimental still. Written almost entirely in polyphonic prose, it is perhaps the most unified of Lowell's
works, the most epic in its reach. Choosing subjects remote from her
in time and place—England, Italy, Japan—Lowell hoped to stress

"the essentially dramatic (or objective) nature of her work" and to keep reviewers from identifying her with the characters and speakers of her poems.[52] Between *Men, Women and Ghosts* and *Can Grande's Castle,* she published *Tendencies in Modern American Poetry*—a critical study of Edwin Arlington Robinson, Frost, Edgar Lee Masters, Sandburg, Fletcher, and H. D. Damon calls *Tendencies* "the most important critical work produced in the United States for many years."[53] In describing three important stages in the rise of the new poetry, it was at least a major contribution to American literary criticism in 1917, and for some years after. The chapter on H. D. and Fletcher provides an overview of the imagist movement, from which Lowell does not omit Pound. In the meantime, the *Some Imagist Poets* of 1915 had been followed by similar anthologies in 1916 and 1917. There would be no more, but Lowell felt that the anthologies had done their work. Poetry sales in America were good, and the demand for modern poetry was growing. When the United States entered World War I, Lowell volunteered to send collections of poetry books to the six training camps in Massachusetts. She soon had requests from camps and hospitals across the country.[54]

Twelve days before *Can Grande's Castle* appeared, Lowell had her first operation for hernia—three more were to follow in the next two years. The condition, which was eventually to kill her, had begun two years earlier, in 1916, at Lowell's New Hampshire summer home. She and Ada Dwyer were driving a horse and buggy down a mountain road when, because of the dark or the rain, the horse became confused, and the hind wheels of the buggy stuck in a shallow ditch. Giving the reins to her friend, Lowell got out and lifted the back end of the buggy onto the road again—tearing, though she did not know it, some muscles in her abdomen and starting an umbilical hernia. That fall she was so seriously ill from overwork—suffering from neuralgia, gastritis, and jaundice—that she was not told for several days of the death of her beloved brother, Percival. She began to suffer from headaches and eyestrain and was in bed again with the flu after Christmas 1917. Though she recovered, her constitution was weakening. In March 1918, unable to sleep, in a New York hotel, she pushed her large bed to a different position. "Suddenly she felt something give and break in her body. The abdominal muscles, strained by lifting the buggy in the summer of 1916, had separated"—two months later she learned she had a genuine rupture.[55] Her first operation, on 12 September, was successful, but it so exhausted her that she spent the rest of the month in bed. Indigestion troubled her; her blood pressure began to rise, eventually reaching 240; then, during a major epidemic in January 1919, Lowell caught the flu again. Her violent coughing must have broken one of the stitches from her operation, though it was not until the end of the year that she noticed an ominous swelling near her wound. Another operation, a more difficult one this time, was scheduled for February 1920.

For the last seven or eight years of her life, Lowell was never entirely well, never enjoyed a prolonged period of uninterrupted health—a fact that makes her productivity during these years all the more remarkable. After the two books of narrative poems—*Men, Women and Ghosts* and *Can Grande's Castle*—in September 1919 she published *Pictures of the Floating World,* a volume of lyric poems, including some of her finest in that form. By then she had begun her work with Florence Ayscough on the Chinese poems that they published as *Fir-Flower Tablets* in December 1921. Every month in 1919 saw something of hers published in one of more than a dozen journals and newspapers. In March, she gave the first lecture by a woman at Harvard—one of her major essays, "Some Musical Analogies in Modern Poetry." In 1920, a year of two difficult operations in February and October, she again published extensively in periodicals, and completed a substantial portion of her sixth book of poems, *Legends* (May 1921), the book that Lawrence thought her best. Between the two operations, she also went on several tours, reading the Phi Beta Kappa poem at Columbia on 1 June; traveled to Waco, Texas, to receive an honorary degree; and undertook to organize an American committee to raise money to buy the house where Keats wrote the "Ode to a Nightingale."[56] Surely, few have accomplished so much under such physical distress.

Lowell never slowed down, apparently never thought of taking a vacation from the work of writing. But her energies were not inexhaustible, and the wrangling over the new poetry began to weary her and sometimes distorted her judgment. She remained loyal to friends like Lawrence, to whom she had given a typewriter in 1914 and some much needed money several times later, but she began to think of those who opposed her or differed from her as conspirators plotting against her. She called Florence Ayscough an "innocent lamb" for not realizing "the rings of intrigue in this poetry business. The more successful I am, the more I am hated. . . . I am having greater proof of it every day. The public is more and more for me, the poets—that is, those less successful than I—more and more against me. I meet with no jealousy from men who have arrived, like Frost, Lindsay, and Sandburg, but I meet with nothing else from those of lower rank."[57] There was some justification for her attitude. The spectrist hoax—a parody of the new poetry perpetrated by Witter Bynner and Arthur Davidson Ficke—almost certainly had her as a prime target.[58] Opponents capitalized on her cigar smoking, her weight, her exacting demands, and there was Pound's derisive taunt of "Amygism." But she was wrong to include Harriet Monroe among her enemies and to tell Florence Ayscough that Monroe "hates me so."[59] Monroe was genuinely fond of Lowell, but was not convinced that she was a great poet. Lowell felt slighted by *Poetry*, overlooked in favor of Pound, and she resented not being given *Poetry*'s highly regarded Helen Haire Levinson prize. The victim of prejudice, Lowell could be unfair herself and less than scrupulous in her efforts to advance her cause. In 1915 she reviewed Fletcher's *Irradiations*, but because the book was dedicated to her, she wanted the review to appear anonymously. After she had written it, the *New Republic* insisted that it be signed. She then asked that the following sentences be placed somewhere in the middle of the review, where they would not be noticeable: "Mr. Fletcher has dedicated his book to me, and it is an honor which I greatly appreciate, but my opinion of Mr. Fletcher's work is too high for it to be silenced by a dedication. I imagine that it is only in America that friendship is considered to deaden the critical faculty." But the sentences were placed conspicuously in the final paragraph, which enraged her.[60] Given Fletcher's praises of her work, her review of his supported the charge that the imagists were a mutual admiration society. At about the same time she was looking forward to a special *Egoist* issue on the imagists, thinking it would help the first *Some Imagist Poets*. The issue, the work of Aldington, was excellent, but when Lowell saw that it contained a critical article by Harold Monro, questioning the claims of imagism and denying that her polyphonic prose "Bombardment" was poetry, she canceled plans to distribute copies in America. Instead, it appears that she and Fletcher reviewed *Some Imagist Poets* themselves, using the pseudonym George Lane. The review praises each of the six poets in the anthology, and calls "The Bombardment" Lowell's "most remarkable poem."[61]

By 1919 Lowell was a considerably better and more successful poet than when she had written "The Bombardment," but the controversies and her illnesses were taking their toll on her. She felt threatened, an obvious target of radical agitators because of her wealth and family connections. Her sheepdogs, a fearsome-looking pack of defenders, had sickened during the war because of meat rationing, and with an immense sense of loss Lowell had to have them killed. After the war she bought a revolver, which she kept near her while she wrote all night. Her nerves were strained, and at a dinner party given in her honor by the Untermeyers, they snapped.

The conversation centered on whether a supposed German spy, George Sylvester Viereck, should be ousted from the Poetry Society. Several guests argued that, since nothing had been proved against Viereck, to take action against him would be to give way to the anti-German hysteria of the times. Lowell had written poems denouncing the Germans during the war, and someone asked her if one of them, "The Cornucopia of Red and Green Comfits," wasn't melodramatic. "Abruptly," according to Jean Untermeyer, "Amy's voice took on an edge of that very hysteria we had been decrying, a tone foreign to her":

You don't know what you're talking about. Times are changing, we're all of us in danger. A lawless element may take over at any moment. It's people like myself that they'll go for. I tell you I feel it. How many nights when I sit writing in my library, nobody awake in the whole house but me and my Winky [her cat], I think I hear intruders—blackguards—and I grasp my revolver, ready to shoot. I feel these things, and I will fight. I am the last of the Barons . . . the last of the Barons!" she shouted, and pounded her small fists on the glass top, the plates rattled, and the maid came running in from the kitchen with round, scared eyes to find out what the commotion was about. But I had seen the dangerous red mount into Amy's usually controlled and alert face, and I had heard that strange note in her voice. I feared an apoplectic seizure.[62]

Mrs. Untermeyer took Lowell into another room to soothe her, and later Lowell apologized. When Lowell and Ada Dwyer had left, the rest of the dinner party excitedly discussed "what had been a really disturbing exhibition."

A different but equally violent scene occurred shortly afterward at the Contemporary Club of Philadelphia, where on 12 November 1919, Lowell read an essay, "Walt Whitman and the New Poetry," in honor of the Whitman Centenary. Lowell gives a balanced estimate of Whitman, admitting his greatness as a visionary American poet, but stressing his limitations too—his inept use of words (inversions, clichés), and particularly his lack of rhythm: "Whitman never had the slightest idea of what cadence is, and I think it does not take much reading to force the conviction that he had very little rhythmical sense."[63] She refuted the notion that modern poets derived their sense of form from Whitman. Her listeners had come to hear Whitman lauded, not put in his place or denied a sense of rhythm, and a fierce argument erupted. One of the speakers following her defended Whitman and attacked modern free verse; another accused her of being a "literary hand-grenade thrower." Then, as she wrote to Sandburg, Lowell "slammed back good and plenty."[64]

The episode made front page headlines in the *Philadelphia Public Ledger* for 13 November, "Tears Punctuate Stormy Spots in Vers Libre Debate." The report tells of Lowell bursting into tears "when criticism was directed against the modern literary school of which she is the leader. In the presence of justices of the Supreme Court, nationally known literati, prominent members of the bar and other persons of distinction, she interrupted the proceedings repeatedly so that the entire program was necessarily changed." Lowell was angry because she had been promised there would be no debate, and because she felt the attacks against her were personal. But she also believed that the uproar had been planned, that it was part of an organized opposition to her. In an interview that appeared in the *Public Ledger* on 14 November, she called her critics "yapping terriers" and firmly denied that she had wept: "I was deeply affected. I was incensed, but there were no tears"—a claim she repeated in several letters to friends. One of her opponents at the meeting refuted her "hysterical accusation that there was a conspiracy to attack her verse" as "ridiculous" and without any basis in fact. He accused her of wanting to be treated as a "sacrosanct personage," expecting "incense from lay acolytes and satelites." The 14 November editorial page, however, had high praise for Lowell's talk as "one of the most delightful and altogether engaging addresses that any society in Philadelphia ever heard. She had her hearers with her at the outset, by the breezy unconventionality of her presence." But it also called the meeting "a head-on collision."

Whatever actually did transpire on the night of 12 November 1919, it was a stormy meeting. Lowell did lose her self-control and was very likely hysterical—a marked difference from the poise with which she parried her hecklers at the Poetry Society four and a half years before. To be so defensive about her work, even as an established poet, perhaps suggests less real confidence in its value than she appeared to have. But she was also tired of fighting, and again she was not well. Jean Gould says that Lowell had a heart attack the night before the Whitman reading.[65] We have seen Jean Untermeyer very rightly concerned about Lowell having a stroke a short time before. The Whitman debate was the last of her public quarrels over the new poetry, but with characteristic drive she went forward in the next few years to her greatest success as a public reader. In her final years, she felt less need to defend free verse and imagism, and she virtually stopped writing polyphonic prose. She usually had good common sense, and she knew that for poetry to remain vital it had to evolve, that a new generation of poets would succeed hers and create its own movements. It did not escape her attention, of course, that the "collision" in Philadelphia resulted in her books being sold out in that city.

Final Years

Until the very end, Lowell did not strike her friends as an invalid, as weakening, but as a storm center, a woman of abundant spirits. Having a hearty sense of humor, she could laugh at her own peculiarities. One story that Gould says Lowell liked to tell about herself stemmed from an argument she had with a mechanic who had fixed her car in a rural area. Not having money with her, Lowell told the man to charge it; but he questioned whether her credit was any good. Lowell told him who she was and that her brother was president of Harvard. When the man questioned that, she told him to call Harvard and find out for himself. She left the garage; the mechanic called and got Lawrence Lowell on the phone, explaining his problem with this strange woman. "What is she doing now?" Lawrence asked. "Sitting across the road smoking a cigar," said the mechanic. "That's my sister," Lawrence said.[66]

She put her comic gifts to use in *A Critical Fable,* a long, witty survey, in rhymed couplets, of the leading poets of her time, including herself, whom she described as a "whirling afflatus." Lowell published the poem anonymously on 15 September 1922. She hoped to set the literary world buzzing over its possible author; and for more than a year—Lowell acknowledged the work early in 1924—various candidates were proposed, with Lowell vigorously suggesting several names. Modeled after James Russell Lowell's *Fable For Critics, A Critical Fable* displays genuine humor, but Lowell intended it as more than just a diversion. She thought it was a better poem than in fact it is, and even while she was stoutly denying that it was hers she was boosting it as "immensely amusing." She even tried, "as chairman of the *Bookman*'s poetry committee, to have the work put on the recommended list for women's clubs."[67] Although most of the portraits give a sincere estimate, made with a lighthearted touch, others—including the lines on Eliot and Pound—give way to bitterness; Lowell's enmity as well as her generosity is apparent; and she cannot resist, under cover of the anonymous voice, predicting future renown for herself.

Lowell wrote *A Critical Fable* while convalescing from her fourth operation, which took place in May 1921; in September, the hernia broke through again. It now took three quarters of an hour, every day, to wrap her in elaborate bandages, and she felt considerable discomfort. Yet she kept close to her normal pace. Besides writing the *Fable,* she completed *Fir-Flower Tablets,* a volume of Chinese poems on which she had been working with Florence Ayscough for four years. Living for most of this time in China, Ayscough sent Lowell literal prose translations of Chinese lyrics, with an analysis of the etymology and connotations of certain Chinese characters. Lowell then used the information to write free-verse poems as close to the originals as she could. The women worked painstakingly, often sending a draft back and forth several times between Brookline and China before both were satisfied.[68] Published in December 1921, too late for the Christmas trade Lowell usually aimed at, *Fir-Flower Tablets* was the culmination of Lowell's interest in the Far East, which began when she was a girl receiving letters and gifts from Percival in Japan. She and Ayscough immediately began plans for a second collaboration.

But an even stronger interest intervened, one that took up the rest of her life and perhaps cost her her life—the biography of Keats. Lowell had been a lover of Keats since the 1890s, when she brought her schoolmates home and read his poetry to them. His influence is strong in her early poetry; the title of her first book, *A Dome of Many-Coloured Glass,* is taken from "Adonais," Shelley's elegy to Keats. Throughout her career, she wrote a number of poems on or about Keats. In her extensive and excellent collection of manuscripts and books, the Keats material was the most important and cherished. Her Keats collection, which contained "the largest amount of unpublished

material in the world," and which was certainly one of the most important in America, included twelve manuscripts and thirty-nine letters.[69] It was through Keats, Lowell said, that she "first learnt to love
poetry, and through the study of his manuscripts that [she] first
learnt how to write it." She felt justified in saying, in a conversation
on 28 January 1921, "I *know* that man's [Keats's] mental processes—
And I *don't believe anybody else does.* That may sound conceited but it
is the truth."[70] The next month she gave the Keats Centenary Address at Yale.

Almost immediately, she decided to make the Centenary essay the
nucleus of a critical biography. Her aims were modest at first. She
would not write an exhaustive biography like Sir Sidney Colvin's, but
a psychological study of Keats's mind and development, and she
wanted to vindicate the character of Fanny Brawne. Lowell hoped to
have the book finished that fall, before *Fir-Flower Tablets* appeared,
but she seriously underestimated the amount of work she had to do.
In February 1922, she again hoped to be done by the fall, when in
fact she was not ready to begin writing until March 1923. Her own
poetry and her tours—she went to Charleston, South Carolina, in
1922—interrupted her; but it is clear that the more Lowell worked
on Keats the more she changed her mind and determined to write an
exhaustive biography. Though not trained as a scholar, she had a
scholar's devotion to thoroughness. She wanted to use as much unpublished, firsthand material as she could get access to. This involved
her in an elaborate cat-and-mouse game with another noted Keats
collector, Fred Holland Day, who possessed thirty-one unpublished
letters by Fanny Brawne to Keats's sister. Lowell badly wanted to
read these, but Day would not let her examine them freely. Instead,
he showed her only selected portions of letters or summarized the
contents for her. Only through an oversight of Day's associate did
Lowell discover that the letters were written to Keats's sister. An ec-
centric, Day kept himself bedridden, so that the ailing Lowell had to
visit him. She flattered, entreated, did everything she could to persuade Day to release the Fanny Brawne letters, only to be over-
matched by Day's stubbornness.

In the meantime she was working feverishly to get the biography
out by 1924—claiming, with more truth than she knew, that the
work was killing her. A welcomed interruption came in the fall of
1923, when Eleonora Duse returned to America. Lowell attended
Duse's performances in New York and Boston, and entertained the

aging actress at Sevenels. When Lowell discovered that Duse lived on practically nothing but champagne, which was difficult to obtain because of prohibition, she emptied her wine cellar and those of her friends and became an impromptu bootlegger, supplying Duse with champagne during the whole of her American tour. She also wrote several memorable poems on the woman who long ago had first inspired her to write poetry. She hoped to persuade Duse to pay her a longer visit, but Duse died suddenly in Pittsburgh in April 1924. Lowell went there to see her body lying in state, and later attended the massive funeral in New York.

Finally, in July, she completed the first draft of Keats. The two-volume biography, more than twelve-hundred pages long, was scheduled for early 1925. She had worked at nothing so long or so hard as at Keats—it drained her energy. She had become so involved with Keats's life and work that she almost felt as if his identity were replacing hers. "My view of anything but Keats is becoming entirely blinded," she wrote Fred Day. "I eat, drink, sleep and talk that man, and pretty soon I shall be signing his name to my letters. I surely had no idea of the task when I began."[71] But she was also very pleased when, in October, she learned that she had at last won *Poetry*'s Helen Haire Levinson Prize, for "Evelyn Ray." In thanking Harriet Monroe, Lowell said that she had not been out of her house that summer more than four times, had not had "even an hour to walk round the place in."[72]

John Keats was a great success. Five days after it was published on 10 February 1925, a fourth printing was ordered. The first two had been sold out before publication. Lowell appeared on the cover of the 2 March *Time* magazine. But the triumph was mixed with bitterness and tragedy too. On the day that Lowell received her advance copies, she learned that her sister, Katherine, had fallen to her death from a hotel window. And while American reviews lauded her biography, British reviews were cooler and more hostile. Lowell had already planned to visit England that spring, and now began to arrange a series of lecture dates to increase interest in the book and gain a fairer hearing for it. She also looked forward to meeting many of the friends she had not seen since 1914—including Thomas Hardy, whom she had met on the eve of the war and corresponded with since. To bid her farewell, and because her fiftieth birthday had passed without much notice the year before, a large group of her friends held a "Complimentary Dinner in Honour of Miss Amy Lowell" on 4 April

1925. Several hundred attended; and Lowell—who, typically, was an hour late—heard herself praised in a dozen speeches. At the end, she read one of her great poems, "Lilacs."

And it was the end. Perhaps the excitement of finishing Keats and of planning her trip concealed from Lowell how truly ill she was. She had no strength left. Eleanor Belmont, a friend who attended the dinner, was "startled to see the change that had taken place" in just two months.[73] Six days after the dinner, her hernia broke through again, with the worst pain and complications she had ever experienced. She lost weight rapidly, and suffered from a constant nausea so that she could not eat or regain her strength. Her blood pressure was high. The trip to England and all engagements were canceled; the doctors prescribed absolute quiet, as even moving about threatened a hernia-strangulation. Risky though it would be, an operation was scheduled for 13 May. On 12 May, while her nurse was wrapping her in the elaborate bandages, Lowell felt her hand go numb; then looking in the mirror, she saw the right side of her face drop. "A stroke," she said to Ada Dwyer. They carried her to the couch, where she died an hour and a half later.[74]

Following her wishes, Lowell's body was cremated, with only her family, her personal maid, Ada Dwyer, and Eleanor Belmont attending the funeral. She left enough uncollected poems for three more books, which Ada Dwyer saw through the press: *What's O'Clock* (1925), *East Wind* (1926), and *Ballads for Sale* (1927). To all but the few who knew how ill she had been, her death came as a shock. It "is like the fall of a dynasty," Elizabeth Sergeant said.[75] Harriet Monroe, with whom Lowell had quarreled and made peace for more than a decade, called her "a great woman, a true and loyal friend, and, in the finest sense of the phrase, a good sport. . . . It seems impossible that a spirit so vivid and vital has left the place she loved, and will speak to us in the flesh no more."[76] In 1926 *What's O'Clock,* containing some of Lowell's best and most mature poems, was awarded the Pulitzer Prize.

Chapter Two
Lowell on the New Poetry: The Critical Prose

In her self-portrait in *A Critical Fable,* Lowell satirizes her penchant for writing aggressive prefaces:

> Every book that she writes has a preface to guard it
> Which spits fire and cannon-balls, making each hard hit
> Tell, and mow down its swathe of objectors.
> But critics have ever been good resurrectors.
> Since she keeps the fight going, they rise to do battle,
> When the whole mess is only so much tittle-tattle.
>
> (C, 411)

More seriously, she felt that the new poetry was often criticized and misjudged by people who did not understand its aims or methods, and who expected poetry to fit the traditional forms they knew. Convinced that a poetic renaissance was taking place, Lowell hoped to show that a new poetry had evolved because new forms of expression were needed, and that the conservatives, who questioned whether imagism and free verse were poetry at all, were wrong. She had firm convictions about poetry, though she never claimed to be an original theorist, and she welcomed the challenge of defending her and her contemporaries' work. Often subjective and impressionistic, sometimes strongly opinionated, Lowell on the whole was a clearheaded, well-informed critic who, in very capable, informal prose, argued for an open-minded approach to the younger, modern poets. She quickly became one of their chief apologists. Probably no one worked harder than she to formulate and defend the rhythmic principles of free verse; certainly few equaled her in ability to generate interest in poetry and to make the new poetry exciting. The history of the poetic renaissance that began in 1912, the feelings it stirred in those who took part in it, would be incomplete and seem less colorful without Lowell's account.

Lowell's prose writings are very extensive. She wrote more than eighty essays, prefaces, and reviews, in addition to three books of biography and criticism: *Six French Poets, Tendencies in Modern American Poetry,* and the two volumes of *John Keats.* A thorough study of her prose would leave little space in which to consider her poetry, the work that Lowell considered her most important. I will concentrate, therefore, on some of the more significant essays and the *Tendencies,* in which Lowell discusses the state of American poetry, explains the manner and methods of the new poetry, particularly imagism, and defines and defends such concepts and terms as "externality," "cadenced verse," and "polyphonic prose." The writings selected contain Lowell's deep-seated beliefs, values, and attitudes—the chief tenets of her *ars poetica;* and they show at times the problems the poets creating a new poetry encountered when attempting to define their new techniques and vision.

The Racial Soul: Lowell on American Poetry

Lowell believed that the new poetry, in all its forms, had broken from the traditions of the immediate past, and that this revolt was especially important and pronounced in America. In fact, a major achievement of the new poetry was the creation of a truly American art, one that reflected the racial characteristics of a people Lowell described as unlike any other. The great names of the nineteenth century—Longfellow, Whittier, James Russell Lowell—were essentially transplanted Britons, colonials copying English models. "We have never had a definite American poetry before," she wrote in "Is There a National Spirit in 'The New Poetry' of America?" Only Poe and Whitman had been "truly American. By this I do not mean that our poets did not write on American subjects, but that they did so in the true English fashion, and a little less well than the poets of the parent stock. Critically, they should be considered rather as English provincial poets than as American poets. We were colonials in everything except Government. Our ideas in all the arts came from England, we acknowledged England to be 'home' in all things spiritual."[1] Even though American subjects alone do not necessarily result in an American art, the American landscape and people had not been adequately treated before the renaissance of 1912—at least not in poetry; presumably Lowell would not consider Melville or Twain provincial writers. The older poets tended to look for beauty and inspiration on the other side of the Atlantic. The younger poets have found that "the Singer Building is an achievement to be proud of and one need not sigh because we are not evolving Parthenons; that the Yankee farmer is as interesting as the Wessex yokel; and that sun, and rain, and cloud are as lyric here as over the orchards of Normandy. It is a great deal to have discovered that" (*I,* 340). Whitman had said much the same thing, which is one reason that Lowell makes him an exception to the prevailing provincialism of his time.

Whitman, however, could identify with all races. Lowell was very conscious of being an Anglo-Saxon, and was as proud of her English descent as she was of her American birth. The massive European immigration that took place during her lifetime brought profound changes to what she felt was the essential Anglo-Saxon character of the American people, changes that sometimes disturbed her. It is Sandburg, a Swede, "and his ilk who are moving us away from our Anglo-Saxon inheritance. It is he and his ilk who bring us the points of view which are working so surely, if insidiously, upon the whole body of the people." The American population has become "a crazy quilt of racial samples" (*T,* 201). She tended to stereotype different races and nationalities. She finds it "interesting to note a certain strain of sentiment in John Gould Fletcher's work, which he undoubtedly inherits from his German and Danish forbears. We can also see a love of the fantastic, a sort of allegorical, elfin quality which links him to these Northern, Teutonic nations" (*T,* 282). The "Flemish character," she confidently reports, "is made up of two parts, one composed of violent and brutal animal spirits, the other of strange, unreasoning mysticism"; brushing aside a long line of French (not to mention Italian and Spanish) saints, she can "hardly believe religion, as we conceive the term, to be possible to the Latin mind."[2] The "we" assumes that her readers do not include Latins, but share with her an American Anglo-Saxon mind.

Racial stereotyping exists today; it was far more common in Lowell's time, however, and it shaped her attitudes, as did her wealth and class. Sandburg's point of view is working "insidiously" upon America because it leads him to champion the poor and the disadvantaged, so that "those least far on the evolutionary road, those least important if we measure by scientific laws, come in for most attention" (*T,* 217). But though they may have limited her, Lowell's notions of the races also gave her an enlarged vision of the growth of American literature. The foreign traits that were entering and changing Anglo-Saxon America were also freeing it from its dependence on English models. "Gradually the attitude of our country changed. Latin and Celtic immigration began to show its influence. We may deny it; we may say that the immigrants were of so low a class that their effect upon the world of ideas must be *nil*. The fact remains. Constant contact with these people had its effect." By the end of the nineteenth century, Americans who traveled abroad went, not to England, but to Italy and France. "They read French, they came in contact with French thought. Insensibly they were modified away from purely British influences"—an essential step, in Lowell's point of view and for all her pride in her own English blood, for the formation of an American race and its appropriate literature (*I*, 340).

A close correlation between race and literature runs throughout Lowell's writings. Until a race has defined or become itself, it will depend largely on the literary models of other nations; yet the development of its own literature is an essential process in the evolution of itself as a distinct race. The new poetry, therefore, is the expression of the new American, who could not fully emerge as such without his own poetry. "The American is a highly nervous race, quick, impatient, energetic. Do we not find all these qualities in a marked degree in the New Poetry? . . . We are a sober and a temperate people, a people of ideals and reticencies, therefore we find here very little of the voluptuousness which is so marked a trait of the poetry of all Latin peoples. . . . We are materialists in a strange, joyful way—loving the things we can see, and hear, and taste, and touch, and smell. So these verses are full of scenes and objects, of beauties—Nature's, Art's—of preoccupation with the things all about us" (*I*, 347). There are, of course, other, different concepts of what is American about America and its art, and Lowell's American still resembles more the New England, Anglo-Saxon Yankee than, say, Vachel Lindsay or some of the Spoon Riverites. Yet she considered Lindsay and Edgar Lee Masters essentially American poets. They wrote in an American idiom, and for Lowell, "Language is more than language; it is the key by which we enter the race-soul" (*T*, 333).

In her most important and extended study of American poetry, *Tendencies in Modern American Poetry*, Lowell uses the work of six poets—Robinson, Frost, Masters, Sandburg, Fletcher, and H. D.— to describe three stages through which American poetry had evolved into a truly national and modern art. In the first stage, older cultural traditions begin to break down, and poets search for new ideas and techniques, although the older traditions still have weight. Robinson and Frost represent the first stage, in their realism and plain, direct speech, but also in their adherence to traditional poetic rhythms and forms. The second stage is revolutionary. Cultural traditions are rejected or challenged, without a new tradition taking their place, and the result is often cynicism and a despair of finding any beauty in life. Masters and Sandburg represent the second stage. Master's preoccupation with sex and crime in *The Spoon River Anthology* and the conflict in Sandburg between pure lyricism and socialist propaganda result in powerful but disturbing poems. The third stage occurs when a new tradition or culture has been formed, when new beliefs and attitudes have replaced the old. Lowell finds this happening in the work of the imagists, Fletcher and H. D. In the first stage, "beauty is a thing remembered and haunting"; in the second, "it is crowded out by the stress of travail, by the pangs of a birth that has not yet occurred"; in the third stage, "it is rediscovered and intoxicating" (*T*, 141).

Like all such schemes, Lowell's breakdown of modern American poetry into three stages suffers from oversimplification; her book, though recognized as important when it appeared, was criticized for omitting such poets as Lindsay and Pound. Also, her choice of imagism as the fruition of America's poetic evolution has to be weighed against her own deep involvement in the imagist movement. She was wrong to accuse Masters of being "more preoccupied with sex than any other English or American author has ever been" (*T*, 174); and she overrated Fletcher. She does not clearly identify the specifically American traits of her six authors; she does not, as Harriet Monroe pointed out, always prove her thesis.[3] Yet the limitations of *Tendencies in Modern American Poetry* do not seriously detract from its importance as a fluently written, clear introduction to the work of six diverse and representative poets. Not hesitating to point out lapses or failures when she finds them, Lowell takes pains to discuss each poet fairly, sympathetically, and from inside the world of his or her particular imagination.

In *Tendencies in Modern American Poetry*, Lowell relies heavily on extensive quotation of poems and tends to keep her strictly interpretive comments brief. The book developed from a series of lectures that Lowell gave in Brooklyn in January 1917, and it is apparent that when she first wrote them she meant to draw upon her very considerable skills as a reader of poetry. Many of her judgments have stood well the test of time. Masters's reputation does largely rest on the *Spoon River* poems. Frost does rank higher than any other poet "in our series." H. D. is nearly perfect in what she does. Surely most critics today would agree with Lowell that poetry and propaganda mix uneasily, and that Victorian discursiveness usually weakens a poem. The irony is that it should be Lowell, who wrote many a long-winded poem, praising brevity, insisting that a writer should know when to stop, and warning others against the prolixity she had such trouble with herself.

Imagism and the New Manner in Poetry

Lowell opens her chapter on Fletcher and H. D. with a long explanation of imagism, her last important discussion of the subject and a summation of what she and other writers had said since the essays by Flint and Pound in *Poetry,* March 1913.[4] As the most controversial form of the new poetry, imagism was the subject of an often rancorous debate. For many poets and critics, the imagists were writing the newest poetry, using the newest rhythms and forms, and for that reason were, depending on one's bias, the most important or the most dangerous of the modern poets. On the other hand, the question of what exactly imagism was or stood for was far from settled—as we saw, the poets themselves, at Lowell's London imagist dinner in 1914, did not have the answer. There was a general tendency—it appears in some of Lowell's essays—to use "imagism" and "the new poetry" as virtually interchangeable or synonymous terms; by 1915, the one invariably suggested the other. Moreover, short, free verse imagist poems looked easy to write, and there soon appeared a number of inferior imagist-imitations, which caused Lowell to stress the difficulty of writing good imagist poetry, while the hostile critics warned that the movement threatened the existence of poetry as an art.

Two attacks on imagism, both appearing in May 1915, particularly disturbed Lowell: Conrad Aiken's "The Place of Imagism," published in America; and Harold Monro's "The Imagists Discussed," published in England.[5] Aiken denies that the imagists have produced any significant poetry, and he accuses them of not practicing what they preach. Instead of hard, exact poems, they write decorative verse, full of superficial descriptions only—a charge that was to follow Lowell throughout her career and after her death. Aiken implies that the imagists avoid the traditional poetic forms because they have not mastered them. Only Fletcher, he says, has a sense of rhythm; the others are "music deaf." For illustration, he refers to a Lowell poem that was inadvertently printed backward, claiming that the "poem flowed quite as well backwards as forwards, and, alas, made quite as good sense."[6] Needless to say, the article infuriated Lowell, who was especially proud of her musical ear and rhythmic sense. It was the Monro article, we saw, that caused Lowell to cancel plans for the American distribution of the *Egoist* issue on the imagists, edited by Aldington. In a carefully reasoned, sometimes witty attack, Monro accuses the imagists of being obsessed with newness, of pursuing change for its own sake, and of having prepared a public for their poetry before writing an adequate poetry. The imagists find excitement in smallness: "They are more concerned effectively to describe their rapid impressions than faithfully to record their abiding sentiments. The passing event and its effect on their minds is everything to them." Quoting H. D.'s "Oread"—a short lyric that was frequently cited as fulfilling the requirements of imagism—Monro protests that the poem "can be said in the minute before lunch." It leaves no impression. "It is petty poetry; it is minutely small: it seems intended to be." He calls Lowell's "The Bombardment" a "confession of failure," since it is not even a poem.[7]

Monro's essay is, in part, a review of the 1915 *Some Imagist Poets,* for which Aldington had written a preface containing the chief principles of imagism. Lowell collaborated with Aldington, and she reprinted the principles in *Tendencies in Modern American Poetry,* though how much of the writing is by her, or Aldington, or possibly one of the other contributors to *Some Imagist Poets,* is unknown. The principles themselves, which provoked so much controversy, "are not new," the 1915 preface states. "They are the essentials of all great poetry, indeed of all great literature."

The preface enunciates the principles in six numbered statements. In *Tendencies in Modern American Poetry,* Lowell summarizes them more briefly: "Simplicity and directness of speech; subtlety and beauty of rhythms; individualistic freedom of idea; clearness and vividness of presentation; and concentration" (*T,* 246). Rather than sounding like a revolutionary platform today, the controversial principles probably describe the work of a majority of twentieth-century poets, from the imagists onward.

But therein lies the cause of much of the confusion that surrounded

imagism: how did the imagist differ from his other contemporary
modern poets? Pound did not make the difference clear when he said
that he wanted imagism to stand for something definite, without
going on to specify what it was to stand for. The 1915 preface
claimed that the imagist principles are the essentials of all great literature. There is little difference—and sometimes the language is
very similar—between Lowell's discussion of imagism in the *Tendencies* and her analysis of the more general "idiom of The New Poetry"
in an essay written at about the same time, "A Consideration of Modern Poetry."[8] The "modern idiom" in poetry is characterized by "suggestion"—which involves use of "the exact word" of the first imagist
principle; "vividness"—or the hard clear poetry of the fifth imagist
principle; "concentration"—the sixth imagist principle; and "externality"—which is an attempt to render particulars exactly, as in the
fourth imagist principle. In effect, as Lowell describes them, imagism
and the modern idiom are one and the same. Having wrested the imagist movement away from Pound, Lowell wanted it to be associated
with herself and the five poets—Aldington, H. D., Fletcher, Flint,
and Lawrence—she had persuaded to join her in the *Some Imagist Poets*
anthologies. But the six of them were too different for imagism to
have an exact meaning when applied to them all, as Pound had fore-
seen. Lowell explains that imagism "refers more to the manner of
presentation than to the thing presented. It is a kind of technique
rather than a choice of subject. 'Imagism' simply means . . . a clear
presentation of whatever the author wishes to convey" (*T,* 244). That
broad a definition does include most modern poetry, not just the
short, image-centered poems of an H. D. To justify her classification
of both H. D. and Fletcher as imagists, Lowell refers to "the wide
latitude within the bounds of imagism" (*T,* 280). It simply was not
possible to extend those bounds as far as she did and be successful in
her attempt to teach her readers how not to make "the blunder of
that recent critic who placed Mr. Frost and Mr. Masters in the Imagist group" (*T,* 248). By grouping poets as diverse as Fletcher, Lawrence, and H. D. in her imagist anthologies, Lowell, perhaps, made
the "blunder" inevitable. She herself shows clearly how H. D.'s poetry differs from that of earlier periods, but not how it differs from
that of Masters.

The failure is not a crucial one. For despite her attempt to do so
in the *Tendencies,* Lowell's primary concern was not to draw exact lines

between the different modern schools, but to show how the new poetry differed from the old—how H. D. and Masters belonged to a movement that set them apart from Tennyson. Lowell used imagism, and its proclamation of a new poetic era, as a rallying point for all modern poetry, but she was more interested in the substance of the new poetry than in its labels. The new poet, imagist or not, assumes a different relation between himself and his reader from that of the past. Chiefly, he does not force his meaning on the reader, but makes use of suggestion: "The invoking a place or character rather than describing it." Rather than making comments in his own person, the modern poet relies on the action of his story to suggest "the commentary, which he expects his reader's mind to supply" (*Co,* 104–5). In an earlier essay on the "new manner" in poetry, Lowell makes the same point more strongly. "If there is one thing which the 'new manner' is more against than another, it is preaching in a poem. And this care not to point a moral is one of the most pronounced features of the 'new manner.' " Readers who turn to poetry for noble thoughts, for consolation for the problems of life, find the new manner to be "cold." But as an art, poetry is "organic" rather than explanatory. "The poetry which is a pepsin to weak intellects to whom crude life is indigestible, has nothing in common with the 'new manner.' 'Noble thoughts,' neat little uplift labels wrapped in the tinfoil of pretty verse, has its place in the scheme of existence, no doubt, but to the modern poet it is anathema. He seeks to give life, the world, as it is, as he sees it, at any rate; and the lesson of his poem, if there be one, must be inherent in the poem itself." The poetic art is a cooperative venture with the reader, who must work out the meaning of the poem himself, without expecting the poet to "bellow it . . . through a megaphone in impertinent asides."[9] Thus, bluntly perhaps, but early and with insight into what writers of the next decade would achieve, Lowell grasped one of the fundamental principles of modernist art.

The new manner in poetry is closely allied to the poets' new vision of the world and their relation to it. Older poets tended to write didactic poetry, or a poetry of cosmic universals, because they saw man as the center of the universe; nature has meaning for them only so far as it corresponds to human moods or thoughts—an attitude that Lowell identified with the pathetic fallacy. Modern poets are interested in "things for themselves and not because of the effect they have upon oneself. The poet of the 'new manner' paints landscapes because landscapes are beautiful, not because they chime with his mood. He tells stories because stories are interesting, and not to prove a thesis. He writes narrative poems because his range embraces the world and is not confined to himself." As opposed to the great literature of the past, in which "man stuck out in high relief," the new poetry "attempts to put man in his proper place in the picture; that is why it is so at variance with the method of the so-called 'cosmic' poet" (N, 124). Though reacting against the excessive subjectivity—the "gigantic ego"—of the late Victorian period, the new poets are still free to write about themselves, as well as about others and nature; but they do not emphasize or insist on the importance of the self. Lowell's position on this is very close to Lawrence's—all things are not radiations "out from me," but exist independently in a "vast whole" of which the self is but a small part.[10]

This poetic treatment and vision of things as independent of the self Lowell called, alternately, "the unrelated method" and "externality." Although the two terms have essentially the same meaning in her criticism, "the unrelated method" refers more to a technique of describing nature, and "externality" to the poet's attitude toward nature. The underlying idea for the terms came from Fletcher, who, in 1913, told Lowell of his hope to write a modern poem depicting the various scenes and objects of London, without in any way identifying himself with them: "Thus the whole city would become re-created in my mind by grasping the objects in it simply as objects and as nothing more." This was what the imagists were trying to do, Fletcher thought, but failed at because they did not write in a form large enough for a major city. Fascinated by the technique Fletcher proposed, Lowell suggested that he call it "the unrelated method."[11] Almost immediately, she began experimenting with it herself.

The unrelated method attempts to reproduce in the reader the sensory impression of objects, as experienced by the poet, but without the intrusion of the poet's personality—the objects themselves, unrelated to the human mind. It delights in color, in pictorial effects, and in word sounds for their own sake. Like imagism, the unrelated presentation stresses clarity and precision; the poet using it "eschews the personal application and gives the thing *per se,* just as it struck on his senses."[12] Lowell used the method in "An Aquarium" to render quick movement and shifts of color—pure sensation, unmediated by thought.

> Streaks of green and yellow iridescence,
> Silver shiftings,
> Rings veering out of rings,
> Silver—gold—
> Grey-green opaqueness sliding down,
> With sharp white bubbles
> Shooting and dancing,
> Flinging quickly outward.
> Nosing the bubbles,
> Swallowing them,
> Fish.
>
> (*C,* 151)

The poem was attacked, Lowell says, "by an otherwise friendly critic for the folly of expecting any one to be interested in an aspect of life from which man was sternly banished, not even being permitted the minor role of reflecting mirror. 'Behold,' said the critic, 'how different is the work of Mr. So-and-So; in his poem on an aquarium, the fish are used as metaphor merely; and in such a connection are interesting.' Poor fish, of no importance except to point a moral to the life of man" (*S,* 140). In refusing to relate the fish metaphorically to man, Lowell treats them objectively or, as she preferred to say, externally. "Externality" is Lowell's term for the modern attitude that leads to stories being told simply because they are interesting, and to poems on natural beauty, without didactic comment or the pathetic fallacy. In effect, "externality" is a theory of poetry that finds expression in "the unrelated method," but it more clearly implies its opposite, "internality": a modern poetry that does not exaggerate the importance of the self, that accepts the otherness of nature, as opposed to the moody, introspective poetry of the 1890s. As Lowell describes it, the externality of the modern poet is like the detachment of a scientist. It stems from "a passionate desire for truth, and a dispassionate attitude toward whatever his search for truth may bring him. He records; he does not moralize. He holds no brief for or against, he merely portrays."[13] This does not mean that the poet is unfeeling, but that his object is aesthetic fitness, the creation of beauty, not morality or the showy display of emotion.

Externality, suggestiveness, an exact, vivid language—these elements of the new poetry, like the imagist principles, were not new. Lowell traced the descent of modern poetry to Blake, Coleridge, Poe, Arnold, and the French symbolists. She anticipated by more than a decade the now standard view of Emily Dickinson as an essentially modern poet. Dickinson's "freedom of idea," vividness, and simple direct speech foreshadow the imagist principles of 1915. And although Dickinson was apparently not familiar with free verse, Lowell believed that she was unquestionably moving in its direction.[14]

Modern Rhythm and Form: Vers Libre and Polyphonic Prose

No aspect of imagism or the new poetry interested Lowell more than its experiments in rhythm, particularly the free verse form. She considered "all forms proper for the writing of poetry," and in her own poems metrical lines and traditional forms are as prominent as free verse. But she also thought that the older forms, though they should not be abandoned, were no longer sufficient for all that the modern poets had to say. If a healthy art was always evolving, experimenting with different forms of expression, then the new poetry's discovery of the possibilities inherent in free verse was of vital importance to the growth of poetry. Again, Lowell did not consider free verse a modern invention. She found free verse in Milton and Blake and Arnold; Coleridge anticipated it in "Christabel"; and French poets had been writing vers libre for several decades. Only the name, not the practice, of free verse was new, and Lowell objected to calling vers libre "free verse."

Like some of the other terms Lowell used and had to defend, *free verse* caused misunderstanding. It became associated with free love, or a dropping of all taboos on subject matter; more irritating was the notion that a poet writing free verse did not have to follow any system or rules of rhythm at all. The "English substitute" for vers libre was "thoroughly misleading," Lowell argued. "I often hear the idiotic sentence: 'Has free verse any laws? But I suppose of course it can't have, or it would not be free.' Excellent reasoning, which shows the supreme folly of logic based upon false premises! 'Free verse' is a term which I, personally, do not like to employ, simply because it means nothing." Vers libre means, literally, "free line"—a line that is not obliged to contain a prescribed number of feet. "The proper English term is really 'cadenced verse'; that is, verse built upon cadence and not upon meter. By 'cadence' in poetry, we mean a rhythmic curve, containing one or more stressed accents, and corresponding roughly to the necessity of breathing" (*S*, 141). Her remarks are taken from an essay published in 1920. For more than five years, she had been making the same points to refute the charge that free verse was really a form of prose chopped up to look like poetry. To show that free verse was poetry, Lowell endeavored to discover its rhythms and to demonstrate how they differed from those of prose. For prose had its rhythms too—Lowell believed that all art was rhythmic.

In an early article, written for *Poetry* in 1914, Lowell argued that the difference between poetry and prose lies in the different lengths of their rhythmic curves—prose has a longer, less pronounced rhythm than poetry—and in their use of the "return," which is much more marked in poetry. Between ordinary prose and metrical verse, however, there are delicate gradations, in which we find prose that is almost like poetry and poetry that is almost like prose. What Lowell calls "metrical prose," for instance, has "a slightly more curved line than is usual in prose, with a return beginning to be felt," and vers libre curves "still more markedly," with a more pronounced return.[15] A trained or attentive ear can detect the subtle differences between these intermediate types, according to Lowell, who does not illustrate or chart the rhythmic curve of any of the lines she quotes. She never was able to define clearly what she meant by the "return," although she calls it "one of the most characteristic traits of verse." It came to mean for her something like a recurring motif or repetitive pattern of image, beat, or word sounds, such as alliteration or rhyme. She later said that she wrote the *Poetry* article "entirely upon intuition," and without psychological training or the proper apparatus. By 1914 she did have a substantial knowledge of contemporary music, though, and her subsequent studies of rhythm convinced her that her intuition had led her to hit upon a truth in the early article, without knowing exactly how she had done so.

In the preface that she wrote for *Some Imagist Poets, 1916,* Lowell defends the imagists against the charge that they have discarded rhythm in their use of free verse. Rhythm is "the most important quality in their technique"; but it is cadenced rhythm, not the rhythm of the metrical foot. Two years had done much to clarify her understanding of the rhythms of free verse, as I believe the following illustration shows—she liked it so well that she quoted it several times afterward, in other essays and in the *Tendencies:*

Suppose a person were given the task of walking, or running, round a large circle, with two minutes given to do it in. Two minutes which he would just consume if he walked round the circle quietly. But in order to make the task easier for him, or harder, as the case might be, he was required to complete each half of the circle in exactly a minute. No other restrictions were placed upon him. He might dawdle in the beginning, and run madly to reach the half-circle mark on time, and then complete his task by walking steadily round the second half to goal. Or he might leap, and run, and skip, and linger in all sorts of ways, making up for slow by going fast, and for extra haste by pauses, and varying these movements on either lap of the circle as the humour seized him, only so that he were just one minute in traversing the first half-circle, and just one minute in traversing the second.[16]

Presumably, a poet writing in strict metrical feet would move at a relatively even speed to complete each half circle; given a minute to do so, he would be halfway to the end in thirty seconds. The vers librist has the same one minute to complete the half circle, but after thirty seconds, he could be at any point along the curve—he dawdles and rushes. Although Lowell does not make specific reference to them here, it is clear that she is drawing upon her knowledge of musical rhythms to explain the cadences of free verse, and the 1916 preface does claim the music of Debussy and Stravinsky as an "immediate prototype" of imagism, The modern poet uses rhythmic devices available to the musician: rests, compensated for by rapid sixteenth-note-like rhythms; lento, moderato, and allegro tempos. He constructs a larger rhythmic pattern than that of a line or stanza, and must rhythmically orchestrate the entire two minutes, the completed circle of which is his poem. In "Stravinsky's Three Pieces 'Grotesques,' For String Quartet," a poem in *Men, Women and Ghosts,* Lowell attempted to "reproduce the effect" of Stravinsky's music by varying the rhythms of her free verse.[17]

As she did in the 1914 article on vers libre and metrical prose, Lowell asserts in the 1916 preface that "there is no hard and fast dividing line between prose and poetry." Prose is not without rhythm, and a chief characteristic of the new poetry was its use of the language and syntax of prose. Yet Lowell also contends that imagist free verse is poetry and not "shredded prose." To find a more exact measure of the gradations between the two, in 1917 she participated in an experiment with William M. Patterson, a professor of English at Columbia, who had her read free verse poems into a machine that photographed sound and allowed him to record the intervals between accented syllables. One of the poems Lowell read was H. D.'s "Oread," which Harold Monro had dismissed as occupying only the minute before lunch. I quote the poem here with the accents and slashes Lowell used to indicate her reading of its stressed syllables and rhythmic units.

> Whirl úp/séa—/
> Whírl/your pointed pínes/
> Splásh/your great pínes/on our rócks/
> Húrl/your green óver us/
> Cóver us/with your póols/of fír/

Patterson's machine measured the intervals between the chief accents in tenths of a second, and the following ten intervals were recorded: "13–22–15–24–13–13–19–13–15–13" (S, 143). [18] The basic rhythm of the poem, as read aloud by Lowell, is thirteen-tenths of a second between the accents, regardless of syllable count, with longer intervals at the end of the lines and some variation within the lines. Lowell considered this finding to be important evidence for her claim that free verse was poetry. The predominance of the 13/10 interval showed a recurring rhythmic pattern that differentiated the lines from the more irregular rhythms of prose, and it supported her notion of the stronger "return" in poetry. Yet, because any number of syllables can occur between the accents, "Oread" is different from traditional metrical verse as well. After further experiments, Patterson came up with seven types of verse and prose, as distinguished by rhythm, and Lowell learned that there was more than one type of free verse, more than one "ultimate particle" to which its rhythm "could be reduced." But she felt she had gained scientific support for her earlier intuitions. The intervals in free verse could be graphed to show rhythmic curves; accents and pauses were timed to correspond to the necessity of breathing or the phrasing of an idea. Poetry did indeed follow a time signature, similar to those used in music.

Lowell knew that her studies were an exploratory step toward the rhythms of free verse, not the final word, and she did much to further our understanding of them. But she also tended to treat the sometimes subjective art of scansion as if it were an exact science. I think we can accept her placement of the accents in "Oread," but she was almost certainly wrong to say that there are "only two stressed accents," rather than three, in this line from Lawrence: "I cried, but no one could hear me" (S, 132–33). Instead of analyzing the complex use of rhythm in a Dickinson poem she merely says, "The first two lines are perfect meter, the third is cadence, the fourth and fifth again are meter, while cadence returns in the sixth and seventh" (Poetry and Poets, p. 106). Surely, if the difference between meter and cadence were that obvious, the efforts Lowell made, over the years, to elucidate it would not have been needed or be justified.

Yet it is almost certain that Lowell could hear the difference. Whether or not she was as "aggressively rhythmic" as she claimed, she was, by all accounts of those who heard her, an excellent reader. The governing principle in her theory of poetry, and one of her deepest convictions, is that poetry is an oral art, that poems are a form of speech and must be heard to be completely understood—rather than use the mail, she often took her poems to editors so that she could read them aloud. "To understand *vers libre*," she said, one must "allow the lines to flow as they will when read aloud by an intelligent reader. Then new rhythms will become evident—satisfying and delightful. For this poetry definitely harks back to the old oral tradition; it is written to be spoken. For we believe that poetry is a spoken, not a written art" (*Co,* 107). Although she trusted too confidently in her ability to hear where accents fall, her insistence that poetry be spoken is one of her most valuable contributions. Lowell not only sought for analogies between poetry and music, but knew that poetry produces its music when it is read aloud, cementing the bond between poet and reader and making experiential the concept that poetic language should be the language people speak. At a time when poetry had become something mostly taken in with the eye— as it remains today—Lowell reminded her readers that poetry was originally addressed to the ear. In one of her essays, "Poetry as a Spoken Art," she points out that, with the rise of printing and the growth of the reading public, "poetry ceased to be chanted, ceased to be read aloud at all for the most part; and the poet has suffered as a composer would suffer whose works were doomed to be rendered by no finer instrument than an accordian." Calling the "auditory imagination" just as important as the visual, she gives practical advice about how to train the imaginative ear and become an effective speaker of poetry.[19]

Lowell often urged her readers to read her own poems aloud, especially those she called, using a name suggested by Fletcher, "polyphonic prose." She found the model for polyphonic prose in her readings of modern French writers, especially Paul Fort, who experimented with alternating between the French alexandrine line and prose. Lowell felt that, without his realizing its importance, Fort had stumbled upon the possibilities of a new verse form. She quotes from his preface to *Le Roman de Louis XI:* "I have sought a style which could pass, at the will of the emotion, from prose to verse and from verse to prose, rhythmic prose furnishing the transition. The verse follows the natural elisions of the language. It is presented as prose, all difficulty of elision disappearing in this form. . . . Prose, rhythmic prose, and verse, are only a single instrument graduated" (*Si,* 294; ellipses in original).[20] As we have seen, Lowell agreed that poetry and prose graduated into each other—rhythmic pattern or curve, not appearance on the page, identified a work as poetic. To be effective, the rhythmic variations that Fort introduced, and that she developed in polyphonic prose, required a basic rhythm to vary from. Fort found his in the alexandrine, the standard line in French verse. Lowell rejected iambic pentameter, the basic meter in English, as too heavy and marked for polyphonic prose. She decided to base her form "upon the long, flowing cadence of oratorical prose"—a form of prose that, like poetry, is meant to be spoken (*Co,* 116). She also worked to enhance the effect of rhymes and other word sounds, and in adapting Fort's experiments to English, she felt she had come up with the only form of the new poetry that deserved to be called "new."

Lowell translates a passage by Fort describing the objects thrown from a castle at an army of besiegers:

Ah! many objects very bruising, cutting, sharpened, whetted, ball-shaped, socket-shaped, granulated, horned, toothed, beaked, of earth, of sheet-iron, of freestone, of iron, of steel, curved, bristled, twisted, confused, everything that was badly used up, moss-grown, rusted, frayed, in thongs, in wedges, hollow, sieved, cross-shaped, screw-shaped, hooked, ringing, grating, whistling and snoring, going humph, ouf, louf, pouf, bring, sring, tringle, balaam, bottom, betting, batar, arara, raraboum, bul, bul, breloc, relic, relaps, mil, bomb, marl, broug, batacl, mirobol, pic, poc, quett, strict, pac, diex, mec, pett, sec, sic, soif, flic, faim, bric, broc, brrrrrr. . . . (*Si,* 448)

Such a passage would have obvious appeal to someone who excelled in public readings and in startling her audience. Lowell considered polyphonic prose to be the most likely form for the modern epic. And with its use of repetition and refrain, its placement of rhymes, alliteration, and assonance, it allowed the poet to work as closely to music "as one can without the quality of tone." "Polyphonic," as Lowell often pointed out, means "many-voiced"—a form that uses all the voices of poetry; "prose" merely refers to the typographical arrangement—the constant changes in rhythm would be confusing if indicated by line-length. Polyphonic prose was—using the word Lowell preferred to describe its structure and effect—an "orchestration."

New rhythms and motifs appear in it like different instruments in a symphony. She speaks of the "full orchestra brass chord" of a passage in her "Bronze Horses," and says of the passage that follows it, "Were I a musician I should give this part to the unaccompanied violins woven across by a single oboe" (*S*, 157).

Damon calls polyphonic prose "the most various and supple poetic form ever devised in English."[21] It has yet to prove itself that. The concept of a verbal orchestra is one of Lowell's most original ideas, but she overstated the possibilities of the form, just as she tended to underrate the rhythmic variety and suggestiveness possible to traditional metrical verse. Her limitations as a critic are not hard to see. She sometimes falls into a circular logic—the "exact word" is the word that describes a thing "exactly"; she too often relies on unsupported generalizations, as if the strength of her conviction were enough to carry her point. Certainly she was wrong to accuse Whitman of not having the slightest idea of cadence and of having very little sense of rhythm. Masters, she says, is "a thoroughly American poet . . . not because he deals exclusively with American subjects," which he does not, but "because he is of the bones, and blood, and spirit of America. His thought is American; his reactions are as national as our clear blue skies" (*T*, 184). That oversimplifies and begs the question, and would not escape censure in an undergraduate paper. Lowell's dogged determination to get polyphonic prose accepted as poetry could not convince even a sympathetic friend, who knew something about poetry: "an intelligent reader may be pardoned if he fails to understand that what is called prose and printed as prose is yet not prose."[22] And despite her campaign against the name "free verse," the term prevails today.

Lowell never pretended to be an original or a profound critic. But neither is she the mere popularizer that she is generally taken to be today, when she is considered at all. Deriving many of her thoughts from other imagists, the French, and Leigh Hunt, she was also able to recognize the importance of certain ideas and trends at a time when they were still confusing to many and offensive to some. Without her support, the imagist movement and the development of free verse would have been very different from what they were, and possibly less far-reaching. If she was wrong about Whitman's sense of rhythm, she had other, valuable insights into his work; and if she exaggerated the merits of Fletcher, she was right about Frost, Sandburg, and Lawrence. Richard Aldington, who at first had objected to

Lowell's inclusion in Pound's imagiste anthology, later took issue with the fashion of writing her off "as a society woman, who would never have been heard of as a writer if she hadn't been a Lowell." That view of her, Aldington says, is unfair. "In Amy there was something of an artist and a real aesthetic appreciation. She could not have felt such enthusiasm for Lawrence and H. D. without it."[23]

In one of her best essays, Lowell goes beyond the specific issues involved in imagism and free verse, to argue for the necessity of an educated imagination and the consequent need to improve the teaching of poetry in schools. Before poetry could be adequately taught— and she was right about its frequently being ill-taught—teachers would have to forget what the critics have said, and come to grips with the poetic art themselves. They "must desert the easy path of historical anecdote, for the difficult one of aesthetic comprehension."[24] Students who are forced to memorize lecture notes, instead of being encouraged to perceive for themselves a poem's meaning and beauty, will learn little of lasting value. She urges public libraries to enlarge their selection of imaginative literature for children, and to make their books more easily discoverable by children who do not come from literary homes, and who therefore do not know what to ask for, or how to interpret the information in card catalogs. She wants children to have a generous selection of fairy tales, but access as well to writers like Dickens, Scott, Longfellow, and Lewis Carroll—and be allowed just to "browse." Thinking it a mistake to confine children to strictly juvenile texts, she argued that a child does not have to understand a poem fully in order to be "captivated" by it and stimulated to further reading—an enlightened view in 1917. Fostering imagination in children was vital to Lowell because she was convinced that imagination was "the root of all civilization," and because she saw in the schools of her time too great a stress on teaching children "to do," too little on teaching them "to think." She knew that without a trained imagination, without knowledge of the humanities, thinking becomes mechanical. Her own thinking never was that. Whether arguing for the proper return of poetry to the schools, or challenging her readers to confront the demands of the new poetry, or just wading into debates, her restless mind quickened the literary consciousness of her time.

Chapter Three
The Early Poetry: Learning the Art

Lowell's earliest poetry has little in common with the new poetry she would later defend in her criticism and illustrate in her major poems. Her first book, *A Dome of Many-Coloured Glass*, published in 1912, does not look forward to imagism, but backward to the traditions of the nineteenth century, to the attitudes and manner of such writers as Keats, Tennyson, and Browning. The title is taken from Shelley's "Adonais." Just before it was published, Lowell learned what Harriet Monroe was doing in Chicago, and shortly afterward she discovered the imagists. She moved rapidly into the modern camp; *Sword Blades and Poppy Seed* (1914) was much more original and less derivative than its predecessor. But the differences between the two have been exaggerated. Lowell developed into a modern poet; she did not suddenly become one, and the appeal of the older traditions never left her. Though *Sword Blades and Poppy Seed* is a better book than *Dome*, its poems are not always superior to those in the earlier book, and both works are uneven. Both present considerable diversity, the result of Lowell's experimental urge to write in various forms on a number of different themes and subjects. *Dome* includes personal lyrics, a collection of sonnets, and children's verse. *Sword Blades and Poppy Seed* ranges from imagistic free verse to rhymed couplets to elaborate stanzaic patterns. It contains sonnets as well as three pieces in polyphonic prose. After her first two books, Lowell arranged her material more carefully and more consistently: narratives and monologues in *Men, Women and Ghosts*, polyphonic prose in *Can Grande's Castle*, lyrics and monologues in *Pictures of the Floating World*. For *Dome*, on the other hand, she had to draw on those poems she had written in the ten years before 1912 that she thought fit to publish. *Sword Blades and Poppy Seed* is made up largely of poems that she had published in periodicals since 1912. And though Lowell divided these into "Sword Blade" poems, supposedly dealing with reality, and "Poppy Seed" poems, supposedly dealing with fantasy, the difference between them is not always consistent or clear. Lowell simply did not have, in these early years, a large enough stock of poems to draw upon to give either book a unified tone or approach.

Nor does either book develop a predominant theme, although several themes appear in a number of poems—loneliness; the pursuit, especially the artist's pursuit, of an unattainable ideal or beauty. Rather, just as Lowell experimented with different rhythms and patterns, so she chose a wide variety of subjects to write about: nature, art, love, her feelings, and the experiences of imaginary characters. Her first two books show her learning the art of poetry and attempting to discover all that she could do with it. In *A Dome of Many-Coloured Glass,* Lowell worked mostly with poetic tools handed down to her by earlier writers. In *Sword Blades and Poppy Seed,* without abandoning those, she began to devise and employ her own—or at least newer and less tried—instruments. Like most beginners, she often handled her tools roughly, and sometimes seemed unaware of her ineffective rhymes or of the need for an image with a cutting edge. At the same time, however, her competence was growing. Memorable poems appear in both of her early books, but much more frequently in the second. Taken together, *A Dome of Many-Coloured Glass* and *Sword Blades and Poppy Seed* show Lowell, if not yet a master of her craft, steadily becoming one.

A Dome of Many-Coloured Glass

D. H. Lawrence once warned Lowell that she wrote best when she followed her own nature, her "genuine" self. "If it doesn't come out of your own heart, real Amy Lowell, it is no good, however many colours it may have."[1] Lawrence had just read *Sword Blades and Poppy Seed;* his remark, however, applies even more to *A Dome of Many-Coloured Glass,* which contains much less "real Amy Lowell" than does her second book. Lowell herself was less than satisfied with *Dome,* even before it appeared. "I have been collecting my poems," she wrote to Carl Engel; "they do seem to me so bad. Barely half a dozen which I like at all."[2] Perhaps she sensed that she had written a derivative book, and had based her poems not so much on her own experiences and perceptions as on the attitudes and conventions of established poets—not merely using traditional rhythms and forms to write in predictable ways about such topics as nature or art, but deriving her very sense of language from the old poetry. She addresses abstract, general concepts, such as "time," which she calls the "Joyless emblem of the greed / Of millions."³ "Before Dawn" speaks directly to "Life"—"Austere arbiter of each man's fate, / By whom he learns that Nature's steadfast laws / Are as decrees immutable" (*C,* 17). Inversions are numerous: "distance dim," "willfulness innate," "joy untold," "towers flamboyant," "decrees immutable"—to list just a few. Occasionally, a line seems taken directly from an earlier poet. "Everything mortal has moments immortal," from "A Winter Ride" (*C,* 5), is almost certainly borrowed from Browning's "One Word More": "Even he, the minute makes immortal, / Proves, perchance, but mortal in the minute." Archaisms, including "perchance," appear in *Dome.* The overall effect is one of literary ornateness and stiffness, a poetic diction far removed from what Lowell later defended as the basis of poetry, the spoken language.

Indeed, Lowell violates almost every principle she would come to defend in her essays on imagism and the new manner in poetry. Instead of an exact, expressive speech, her early poems make free use of clichés and forced rhyme; instead of suggestiveness and a muted authorial voice, there is direct moralizing and intrusion by the author. "Roads," for example, describes a landscape that she knew well, most probably a scene near her summer home in New Hampshire. Instead of making us see a distinct place, however, Lowell generalizes and uses exotic trimmings.

> I know a country laced with roads,
>   They join the hills and they span the brooks,
> They weave like a shuttle between broad fields,
>   And slide discreetly through hidden nooks.
> They are canopied like a Persian dome
>   And carpeted with orient dyes.
>   . . . .
> They are set in my heart to a pulsing tune
>   Gay as a honey-bee humming in June.
>
> (*C,* 10)

Ultimately, the roads lead to "fairyland," taking the speaker to "the opaline gates of the Castles of Dream."

The problem with "Roads" and with poems like it is that they are too easy to write and offer little more than an exuberant response to nature. The "brooks/nooks" and "tune/June" rhymes are amateurish at best, as is the image of the heart as a gay, humming bee. The scene is more fanciful and literary than real. A country "canopied like a Persian dome / And carpeted with orient dyes" reflects landscapes that Lowell read about in books, not the New England sky and land that she saw.

In "Teatro Bambino," the poem that follows "Roads," an Italian theater in New Hampshire gives rise to a reverie about Pan:

> What sound is that which echoes through the wood?
>   Is it the reedy note of an oaten pipe?
> Perchance a minute more will see the brood
>   Of the shaggy forest god, and on his lip
> Will rest the rushes he is wont to play.
>
> (C, 11)

In a poem that does not explore the continuities between past and present, Pan's appearance is arbitrary, and to describe him Lowell uses a worn-out, artificial poetic diction: "reedy note," "oaten pipe," "wont to play," "shaggy forest god." As Lowell sinks deeper into her reverie, she imagines that the pines have changed into cypresses; the thrush becomes a nightingale, who bursts "his little heart with anguish." That is precisely the kind of overwriting and falsification of nature that Lowell would soon criticize as the pathetic fallacy. Now and throughout her career, Lowell was drawn to, her imagination stimulated by, foreign scenes and earlier times. She learned to write beautiful poems about places she had never seen; but she also learned not to force a symbolic value on them or drag in mythological trappings she had little interest in. Deliberately to substitute an exotic for a native bird may not violate any artistic principle, but it shows how far Lowell was from her recognition, a few years later, "that the Yankee farmer is as interesting as the Wessex yokel; and that sun, and rain, and cloud are as lyric here as over the orchards of Normandy."[4]

Perhaps the poem furthest removed from the language and syntax of prose, from the new poetry and twentieth-century American speech, is one of the sonnets, "To John Keats":

> Great master! Boyish, sympathetic man!
>   Whose orbed and ripened genius lightly hung
>   From life's slim, twisted tendril and there swung
> In crimson-sphered completeness; guardian
> Of crystal portals through whose openings fan
>   The spicéd winds which blew when earth was young,
>   Scattering wreaths of stars, as Jove once flung
> A golden shower from heights cerulean. . . .
>
> (C, 21)

If Lowell meant to imitate Keats's most ornate style, she succeeds only in writing an unconscious parody of it. Most of Lowell's early sonnets read like belabored exercises that she forced herself to finish, and suffer from the contortions and artificiality that mar this one, although Lowell did not often indulge in such extreme affectations as "crimson-sphered completeness" or "heights cerulean." But perhaps the greatest failing of "To John Keats," and of the other sonnets and lyrics like it, is that it is dull—which the "real Amy Lowell" was not.

Such failings as I have noted, however, serve as a reminder that *Dome* was a beginner's book. Too often in it, Lowell attempted to sound "literary" and to parade her knowledge of traditional poetry. But even in one of her earliest written poems, she was able to speak of a subject that concerned her closely, in language that registers genuine emotion and thought. "The Boston Athenaeum," the longest poem in *Dome,* was probably written in 1903, when Lowell campaigned against a proposal to move the library to a new site. Lowell loves the old books on the old shelves, and as she writes about them she discovers in them a link with her forebears, who governed the Athenaeum and helped to build its collection:

> Our fathers' fathers, slowly and carefully
> Gathered them, one by one, when they were new
> And a delighted world received their thoughts
> Hungrily; while we but love the more,
> Because they are so old and grown so dear!
> The backs of tarnished gold, the faded boards,
> The slightly yellowing page, the strange old type,
> All speak the fashion of another age;
> The thoughts peculiar to the man who wrote
> Arrayed in garb peculiar to the time;
> As though the idiom of a man were caught
> Imprisoned in the idiom of a race.
>
> (C, 22)

Here, rather than the general impressions she is often satisfied with in her landscapes, Lowell particularizes. And as opposed to the mythological machinery of "Teatro Bambino," she explores the relationship between present and past, living reader and dead author, who unite in the books that touch their separate lives:

> And as we read some much-loved masterpiece,
> Read it as long ago the author read,
> . . . .
> We know a certain subtle sympathy,
> We seem to clasp his hand across the past. . . .
>
> (C, 23)

Written, as Foster Damon says, for propaganda, "The Boston Athenaeum" transcends the topical issue of the library's removal to speak of one of the fundamental experiences of reading, of meeting imaginatively the mind within a book.[5]

Several poems in *Dome* deal with the relationship between art and nature. "A Japanese Wood-Carving" describes and reenacts the process by which a tree in a thick forest became a work of art at Sevenels. The carving, a seascape, brings nature's vastness into Lowell's "quiet, firelit room" (C, 4). In "The Green Bowl," occasioned by a present from a nephew, nature and art fuse:

> This little bowl is like a mossy pool
> In a Spring wood, where dogtooth violets grow
> Nodding in chequered sunshine of the trees;
> A quiet place, still, with the sound of birds,
> Where, though unseen, is heard the endless song
> And murmur of the never resting sea.
>
> (C, 7)

Besides showing that Lowell was already capable of an exact, expressive language, the lines develop a complex interdependence between nature and art. The bowl becomes the pool it reminds Lowell of, as well as a "chalice" in which nature and art combine. The leaves carved on its rim replace the leaves of the flowers picked from the woods, so that the artist's leaves on the bowl and the natural flowers in the bowl become one plant—and one work of art.

Two of these early poems are especially important as autobiographical records of Lowell's state of mind before she became known as a poet. "A Fairy Tale" opens with Lowell's memory of reading fairy tales before the glowing fireplace in her nursery when she was a child. Her imagination would build imposing castles in the coals. As trumpets sound, a large crowd files in to attend a christening. Everyone brings precious gifts for the royal child but "one unbidden guest / Who cursed the child and left it bitterness." The second half of the

poem returns to the present and the stark fulfillment of the curse in
real life:

> But overshadowing all is still the curse,
> That never shall I be fulfilled by love!
> Along the parching highroad of the world
> No other soul shall bear mine company.
> Always shall I be teased with semblances,
> With cruel impostures, which I trust awhile
> Then dash to pieces, as a careless boy
> Flings a kaleidoscope, which shattering
> Strews all the ground about with coloured sherds.
> So I behold my visions on the ground
> No longer radiant, an ignoble heap
> Of broken, dusty glass. And so, unlit,
> Even by hope or faith, my dragging steps
> Force me forever through the passing days.
>
> (C, 13)

Lowell seldom revealed her feelings so openly. Her loneliness, her
need for one intimate friend, her repressed and frustrated sexual longings—these had tormented her since her school days, and the admission of them gives a different image of her from the more popular one
of a doughty, self-confident poet-businesswoman. She has gained sufficient power over words to speak of her deep fears and needs with a
clarity and a passion that transcend self-pity, and that make the loss
of youthful illusions and the awakening to an isolated self-consciousness a tragic fall from innocence.

The honesty and depth of feeling in "A Fairy Tale" contrast with
the more artificial hopes and melancholies of many of the other poems
in *Dome*. Its unlit despair is the antithesis to the colored dome of the
volume's title. Shelley's dome of many-colored glass is the thin barrier of life between mankind and eternity, which death breaks
through to make the soul one with the eternal. Therefore, Shelley
says, we should not mourn Adonais, who has died, but aspire to his
state:

> The One remains, the many change and pass;
> Heaven's light forever shines, Earth's shadows fly;
> Life, like a dome of many-coloured glass,
> Stains the white radiance of Eternity,
> Until Death tramples it to fragments. . . .[6]

However imperfectly life may reveal the eternal, as a dome of colored glass it makes us aware of the eternal. Lowell, essentially an agnostic, had no such faith in a life beyond this life, even in Shelleyan terms. In "A Fairy Tale," she replaces Shelley's dome with a kaleidoscope, a child's toy and literally a circle of colored glass, which a careless boy shatters on the ground. A deceptive image of oneness breaks into fragments, leaving Lowell isolated and unloved in a world of many, without any hope of the many becoming one. Ahead of her is a vision of darkness, not light—time's dragging mechanical march, rather than radiant eternity. "A Fairy Tale" is essentially a counterromantic poem in a book of poems largely inspired by the romantics; for it is not only fairy tales and the world of her imagination that Lowell must leave behind her in childhood, but a romantic symbol, a promise, that has been reduced to bits of glass.

The second important autobiographical poem, which also makes creative use of derived material, is "To Elizabeth Ward Perkins." Bessie Ward was an old friend and a Catholic with whom Lowell used to debate religious questions. Here she continues the discussion, writing as one who would like to believe in her friend's religion, but cannot:

> Dear Bessie, would my tired rhyme
> > Had force to rise from apathy,
> > And shaking off its lethargy
> Ring word-tones like a Christmas chime.
>
> But in my soul's high belfry, chill
> > The bitter wind of doubt has blown,
> > The summer swallows all have flown,
> The bells are frost-bound, mute and still.
> . . . .
> The rope I pull is stiff and cold,
> > My straining ears detect no sound
> > Except a sigh, as round and round
> The wind rocks through the timbers old.
> . . . .
> Beneath my feet the snow is lit
> > And gemmed with colours, red, and blue,
> > Topaz, and green, where light falls through
> The saints that in the windows sit.
> . . . .

> Silent and winter-killed I stand,
>   No carol hymns my debt to you;
>   But take this frozen thought in lieu,
> And thaw its music in your hand.

(C, 13)

Lowell's debt, this time to Tennyson, is readily apparent: the stanza
form is taken from *In Memoriam,* as are the Christmas season and the
yearning for a religious consolation that is no longer possible or certain. But Lowell's poem is not just an echo of Tennyson's. Her "win-
ter-killed" vision is closer to the post-Victorian grimness of Thomas
Hardy. Like Hardy, Lowell cannot entirely abandon a religion that
has not kept pace with her modern world, and she feels the "ache" of
those who have lost their faith without finding a substitute for it.
Though keenly aware of what religion offers, Lowell is already above
the church, at once liberated and trapped in its cold bell tower. She
renders the paradoxes of her situation through details of setting and
action. Her more advanced thought has lifted her to a spiritual desolation, has surrounded her with ice, until she becomes a bell-ringer
who pulls a frozen rope and hears only the wind. Even art, her
rhymes, is apathetic, frozen, and cannot ring words in place of the
bells or release its music until—in a beautiful image—it is thawed in
the hands of Bessie Ward below. The modern vision of Lowell's art
is still dependent on the faith, the communal myth, it has separated
her from.

   In effect, Lowell has gone beyond Shelley's dome—the snow *below*
her is colored by the stained glass windows. But here, even more than
in "A Fairy Tale," leaving illusions behind for a vision of reality isolates the seer within her self, rather than uniting her with an eternal
oneness. Ada Dwyer's entry into Lowell's life would end the loneliness expressed in "A Fairy Tale"; "To Elizabeth Ward Perkins" presents the more tragic dilemma of one who has ascended to a point of
vision that does not reveal anything to compensate for what she has
lost in getting there.

Sword Blades and Poppy Seed

   Lowell developed considerably in the two years between *A Dome of
Many-Coloured Glass* and *Sword Blades and Poppy Seed,* and her second
book of poems brought her much attention and acclaim.[7] But though
her work is now more original than it had been, some of the earlier

amateurish mannerisms remain. She seems addicted at times to hackneyed or obtrusive rhymes. The contrived, obvious allegory of "The Coal Picker," in which we learn that the poet must work in dirt and darkness to release his vision, shows her forcing herself to write while uninspired and even uninformed about the conditions she describes. New problems arise. Lowell is now writing longer poems, not all of which justify their length. "The Shadow," which treats one of Lowell's favorite themes, the artist's pursuit of a cold, unattainable ideal, is a monotonous story of a watchmaker who falls in love with a mysterious shadow. He spends the rest of his life in futile attempts to elicit a response from the shadow. Occupying four and a half double-columned pages of *The Complete Poetical Works,* the poem does not reveal the watchmaker's motives or suggest that the shadow is worth pursuing at all.

But even in these unsuccessful attempts Lowell has made an important advance in her art. Much more than she did in *Dome,* she is now experimenting with dramatic and narrative poetry, exploring characters and personalities very different from her own. In "After Hearing a Waltz by Bartok," the speaker is a man who has murdered his rival for a woman. He relives the scene, obsessed by its violence and haunted by his memory of holding the bleeding body of his victim, while the sound of waltz music and dancers intrudes from another room:

> But why did I kill him? Why? Why?
>   In the small, gilded room, near the stair?
> My ears rack and throb with his cry,
>   And his eyes goggle under his hair,
>   As my fingers sink into the fair
> White skin of his throat. It was I!
>
> I killed him! My God! Don't you hear?
>   I shook him until his red tongue
> Hung flapping out through the black, queer,
>   Swollen lines of his lips. And I clung
>   With my nails drawing blood, while I flung
> The loose, heavy body in fear.
>
>   (C, 56–57)

Though he has ridden ten miles from the scene, he still hears the waltz rhythm pounding within him, and in his imagination he is still locked in a grotesque dance of death with his victim. With its

graphic violence and frenzied voice, and with the recurring thump in
the final stanzas of "One! Two! Three!"—the dance music internalized into a death count—the "Waltz by Bartok" is well-adapted for
public readings, and Lowell almost certainly performed it with a
flourish.

What "After Hearing a Waltz by Bartok" lacks, however, is subtlety. In the later stanzas especially, the lines bang at the reader, and
the language becomes shrill and histrionic rather than expressive of
the psychology of violence.

>   One! Two! Three! Give me air! My God!
>   One! Two! Three! I am drowning in slime!
>   One! Two! Three! And his corpse, like a clod,
>   Beats me into a jelly! The chime,
>   One! Two! Three! And his dead legs keep time.
>   Air! Give me air! Air! My God!
>
>   (C, 57)

To employ a musical analogy, as Lowell often did, the numerous ex-
clamations are like an incessant clashing of cymbals—a din of noise
rather than a resolution or heightening of theme. Except that he is
obsessed with his crime and psychologically chained to his victim,
facts established early in the poem, there is little inward revelation of
the speaker's character. His voice keeps to a few strident tones, and
his crime is belabored and overwritten rather than probed.

A much more successful poem, as well as the longest and one of
the most ambitious Lowell had yet written, is "The Great Adventure
of Max Breuck." It presents another version of the pursuit of an ideal
or shadow. Max Breuck, a lawyer in Amsterdam, is summoned from
his friends in a tavern to witness an agreement between one Cornelius
Kurler, a naval merchant, and his creditor, Grootver. Kurler proposes
to pay Grootver the money he owes him after a two-years trading
voyage; if he has not returned in that time, Grootver has his permission to marry his beautiful daughter, Christine. Max Breuck promises
to protect Christine while her father is absent, and the two young
people meet frequently in the Kurler's garden of tulips and fruit
trees. Before long Max is in love, though he keeps their relationship
an honorable one. But when two years have elapsed and Grootver
claims Christine, now "a woman grown," as his bride, Max an-
nounces his love and asks Christine to marry him immediately, thus
foiling Grootver. When they return to Christine's home after their

marriage, Max insists on telling Grootver what they have done, assuring Christine that he will be gone only an hour. But on his way, he meets his old friends, whom he has hardly seen in the past two years, and they insist on his joining them in the tavern from which his adventure started. When Max becomes almost violent in his efforts to leave them, the friends apologize for the joke they have played on him. Max could not possibly be married, they say, because he has never left the tavern; it is not two years from the time they were together last, but the same night. Before Max had entered, someone had filled a pipe with drugged tobacco and given it to him. The drug induces a deep sleep in which years pass as seconds and dreams become as vivid as reality. Disbelieving his friends, insisting that Christine is real, Max rushes to her home to find no trace of it or Christine. Unable to live without her, Max kills himself.

As the synopsis indicates, there is considerable action in this poem, a series of interlocking events, rather than just one scene essentially repeated, as in "The Shadow." A number of minor characters give the narrative color and diversity, and setting is used with considerable effect, as Lowell contrasts the smoky decadence of the tavern with the rich beauty of Christine's tulip garden. In the following stanza, Max sees the garden for the first time, after accompanying Christine to her home:

> The little apple leaves above their heads
> Let fall a quivering sunshine. Quiet, cool,
> In blossomed boughs they sat. Beyond, the beds
> Of tulips blazed, a proper vestibule
> And antechamber to the rainbow. Dyes
> Of prismed richness: Carmine. Madder. Blues
> Tinging dark browns to purple. Silvers flushed
> To amethyst and tinct with gold. Round eyes
> Of scarlet, spotting tender saffron hues.
> Violets sunk to blacks, and reds in orange crushed.
>
> (C, 49)

With her own beautiful garden at Sevenels, Lowell is on firm ground in the world of flowers and trees, and the orchestration of colors here has a solid specificity. It is vital to the poem that the dream be experienced as reality, and that the reader not doubt his senses any more than Max does. The sensuous richness of the garden also foreshadows and parallels Max's love. When he rushes back in his terror, the first thing he finds missing is the garden. And though the descriptions lengthen and slow the narrative—the stanza above is one of six about the garden—such elaboration contributes to the sense of real time passing at a credible pace. When it is necessary, moreover, Lowell changes narrative speed, mixing detailed, slow-moving scenes with rapid summary. Even the stanza form—which is similar to that of Keats's great odes, and which combines the quatrain of the English sonnet and the sestet of the Italian—is handled with ease.

But Lowell shows the greatest skill in the poem when she needs it most, at the scene of Max's awakening. When Max is told that he has been dreaming, the reader must not dismiss his adventure as *only* a dream, which would trivialize the poem. Lowell anticipates this response and prevents it by the actuality with which she invests the dream, but even more so by the emotional power and tension that build to the climax of the awakening. There is no hint that Max has been dreaming when his friends force him back into the tavern, where the scene is dominated by his anger at being kept from Christine. The transition out of Christine's world is both gradual and harrowing.

> Forcing himself to steadiness, he tried
> To quell the uproar, told them what he dared
> Of his own life and circumstance. Implied
> Most urgent matters, time could ill be spared.
> In jesting mood his comrades heard his tale,
> And scoffed at it. He felt his anger more
> Goaded and bursting;—"Cowards! Is no one loth
> To mock at duty—" Here they called for ale,
> And forced a pipe upon him. With an oath
> He shivered it to fragments on the earthen floor.
>
> Sobered a little by his violence,
> And by the host who begged them to be still,
> Nor injure his good name, "Max, no offence,"
> They blurted, "you may leave now if you will."
> "One moment, Max," said Franz. "We've gone too far.
> I ask your pardon for our foolish joke.
> It started in a wager ere you came.
> The talk somehow had fall'n on drugs, a jar
> I brought from China, herbs the natives smoke,
> Was with me, and I thought merely to play a game."
>
> (C, 53)

The exact moment of Max's awakening is uncertain—presumably it occurs when he is once again aware of himself sitting in the tavern. In one sense, of course, he never awakens; dream has replaced reality, or the meaning of the two has changed. The reader, whom Lowell has fooled as thoroughly as Max was, feels the same crushing blow of the truth, and hopes with Max that the story of the drugged tobacco is "a lie." With little overwriting, rather with cold, appalling logic, the awakening scene has compelling dramatic suspense and impact.

There is, on the other hand, a good deal of melodrama in the final scene, when Max rushes from where Christine's house used to be, to a pawnbroker's, and then out along the dykes with a pistol in his hand. "His mind, half-clear, / Babbled 'Christine!' A shot split through the breeze. / The cold stars winked and glittered at his chilling corpse" (*C,* 55). Though she has told the bulk of her story with considerable skill, Lowell has by no means perfected her narrative gifts. She tends to rely in most of her narratives on a violent ending—murder or suicide—or on scenes of heavily charged emotion. A highwayman is captured and hanged; a farmer starves himself to death; a "foreigner" kills several men in a sword fight; the speaker in the "Bartok" poem graphically relives the strangling of his rival—all of which border on and sometimes cross into sensationalism. "In a Castle" ends with a man discovering his wife and one of her lovers, both beheaded, with the body of a second lover who had executed them before killing himself. Other poems meant to be dramatic are overly sentimental, sheer appeals for pity. A young boy earnestly prays for the safe return of a sailor who befriended him. The boy has no one else and promises to devote his life to the Blessed Virgin if the sailor returns, but apparently his prayer goes unheard. "The Forsaken," another appeal to the Virgin, is the monologue of an unwed, pregnant girl, whose parents would reject her if they knew she was pregnant, and who has nowhere to go and is very weary. When it appeared, "The Forsaken" provoked controversy because Lowell used the word *whore* in it. Today, the poem is open to criticism because Lowell was too easily satisfied with a one-dimensional, self-pitying stereotype of a figure that other writers—Hardy, for instance—had treated with more insight and truth.

"The Forsaken" is one of three poems in *Sword Blades and Poppy Seed* written in polyphonic prose. As we have seen, Lowell argued that polyphonic prose was the only distinctively new contribution of the new poetry. She believed it was the only form in which the three poems could be written.[8] In "The Forsaken," however, instead of the fluidity and great variety of treatment Lowell claimed for polyphonic prose, there is wordiness, cliché, and mawkishness. Nor is it evident why "The Forsaken" could not have been written in standard verse form. "In a Castle" is essentially a prose vignette, into which Lowell inserts rhymes and poetic rhythms. It is sensationalistic—two murders and a suicide—but Lowell also uses irony well when the would-be adulterer finds his lover in bed with another man, forcing him to assume the role of the injured husband he had intended to wrong. The narrative switches abruptly from his realization that the other two are in a hidden room to a description of the three mutilated bodies. The third polyphonic prose poem, and the one that makes most use of the potentials of the form, is "The Basket." It is also one of the most difficult and obscure poems in *Sword Blades and Poppy Seed.*

A story of intense, unrequited passion, "The Basket" is broken into five sections—fragments or phases of a relationship that develops swiftly and starkly to a violent climax. As an example of Lowell's early attempts at polyphonic prose, section 1 introduces us to the characters, Peter and Annette, before they are lovers, and to the poem's dominant images: silver moonlight, a roof that glitters like ice, and crimson geraniums.

> The inkstand is full of ink, and the paper lies white and unspotted, in the round light thrown by a candle. Puffs of darkness sweep into the corners, and keep rolling through the room behind his chair. The air is silver and pearl, for the night is liquid with moonlight.
> See how the roof glitters, like ice! . . .
> He has forgotten the woman in the room with the geraniums. He is beating his brain, and in his ear-drums hammers his heavy pulse. She sits on the window-sill, with the basket in her lap. And tap! She cracks a nut. And tap! Another. Tap! Tap! Tap! The shells ricochet upon the roof, and get into the gutters, and bounce over the edge and disappear.
> "It is very queer," thinks Peter, "the basket was empty, I'm sure. How could nuts appear from the atmosphere?"
> The silver-blue moonlight makes the geraniums purple, and the roof glitters like ice. (*C,* 58)

Lowell hoped that rhymes would add musical or tonal richness to polyphonic prose, and she positioned her rhymes at the beginning and in the middle of sentences, as well as at the end, so they would be less pronounced than in regular verse. Nonetheless, the rhymes are often obtrusive and sometimes seem to serve no other purpose than to justify Lowell's claim that polyphonic prose was a form of poetry. On the other hand, the staccato rhythm and sound of the cracking nuts effectively contrasts with the longer, smoother lines describing the night "liquid with moonlight"—and, in fact, the quiet stillness of Peter's life is about to be broken as easily as the shell of a nut. More important still is Lowell's handling of the images, which recur throughout the poem as symbolic motifs: the icy roof enclosing and emphasizing the deep red of passion. Peter crosses the roof to reach the geranium woman, Annette, whom he woos with ardent sexual desire. She, though the geraniums are her symbol, feels none of the passions she arouses, but is cold and chaste like the ice, and she repulses Peter. As his need for her "burns" him, Peter's world, his perception, becomes filled with the color of red. In the nightmarish climax of the poem, he awakens to find the sky seemingly lit by blood, not the moon; it is dripping blood: "And the drops sizzle on his bare skin, and he smells them burning in, and branding his body with the name 'Annette.' " He has become branded with the crimsom color, with the object of his sexual desire, and perhaps, in imagination or dream, he has shed Annette's hymenal blood. Fully awake, however, he sees that it is not blood lighting the sky but flames. The once icy roof is "scorching." At the end, the air is silvery again and liquid with moonlight, but the house, the site of Peter's passion, is a ruin that "glistens, like a palace of ice." The moonlight shines into the blackened holes of two windows, and in the moonlight, staring back at him, Peter sees eyes of geranium red—Annette's. The symbol of passion, lit and enclosed again by a chaste light, haunts passion's ruins.

The lovers' roles are reversed. As Peter had once observed Annette, she now watches him. But she has become a pair of eyes because she eats eyes. The basket that Peter had first imagined to be filled with moonlight, and then thought was filled with nuts, contains human eyes—"hundreds of eyes": "Unwinking, for there are no lids. Blue, black, gray, and hazel, and the irises are cased in the whites, and they glitter and spark under the moon. The basket is heaped with human eyes. She cracks off the whites and throws them away. They ricochet upon the roof, and get into the gutters, and bounce over the edge and disappear. But she is here, quietly sitting on the window-sill, eating human eyes" (*C,* 59). She has already, as it were, consumed Peter's gaze, absorbing him into herself, while she throws off

his passion as easily as the shell of a nut or an iris. Immediately after
the grotesque revelation of the basket, Peter awakens to the blood-
filled sky. Directly above him, not moving, is an eye. Peter escapes
by crossing the roof: "he ricochets, gets to the edge, bounces over
and disappears" (C, 59)—as if he were one of the broken eyes cast off
by Annette.

Complicating the symbolism further, both Peter and Annette are
artists—he is a poet; she embroiders religious vestments and cloths.
Annette, who at first inspired Peter with the title for a book, soon
distracts him from his work; his love for her becomes more important
than his poetry. "I cannot feed my life on being a poet," he tells her
when she has repulsed him again. Annette causes Peter to abandon
the world of art for the world of life, while she lives entirely in and
for her work, her art. She "only understands the ways of a needle
through delicate stuffs, and the shock of one colour on another"
(C, 59). She wants only a red to match the color of her geraniums,
which color appears in the bloody sky at the climax of Peter's love,
and which color she becomes when she stares down at him, the dispassionate occasion of passion, a pair of geranium eyes. Lowell is almost certainly portraying the exacting nature of art in the person of
Annette, and constructing a parable by which Peter learns of its demands. Art arouses passion while remaining free of it; it sacrifices a
house, a relationship, for the sake of a color, a symbol. And it feeds
on human experience—"I must have sight," Annette says, before
Peter sees her eating the eyes and before he becomes like the discarded shell of an eye. Ironically, the poet who cannot live on poetry
alone becomes caught up in the self-contained world of art, a victim
of Annette's total dedication to art. As Peter becomes more vulnerable, more distraught, more human in his need for her, Annette with-
draws into herself. At the end, when she is a pair of geranium-red
eyes, she has become her own work of art, fusing vision with its object—but not joining art to life. Unlike the union of the two in "The
Green Bowl," art and life remain separate, even antagonistic and
competitive in "The Basket." Annette sacrifices life to art and becomes a purely symbolic, disembodied sexual presence to Peter, who
had sacrificed art for life.

My reading of "The Basket" is speculative. "The Basket" is not
only a complex poem, but a confusing one. Damon calls it "a symbolic puzzle."[9] But in its suggestiveness, reliance on symbol, and surrealistic action, it is a far more challenging poem than Lowell's work

of two years earlier. The differences between her first two books, although they are sometimes exaggerated, should not be minimized either. Lowell has clearly extended her range and begun to break free of the older conventions. Her symbolic use of the eye anticipates its importance as a sexual symbol in Peter Shaffer's *Equus.* Polyphonic prose allowed her to experiment with different rhythmic units and with image clusters. And if polyphonic prose never became all that Lowell hoped it would, it gave her a form for which she had practically no models and thus helped her to become a more original writer, a poet more committed to finding original modes of expression.

But Lowell's most important discovery in these earlier years was free verse, which opened her ear to the rhythms and syntax of the spoken language as a proper idiom for poetry. The concentration and unity, the use of strong, spare language, which she found in the imagists, virtually transformed her as a lyric poet. Some of the short, personal lyrics in *Sword Blades and Poppy Seed,* such as "The Taxi," fall just short of her best work in this kind.

> When I go away from you
> The world beats dead
> Like a slackened drum.
> I call out for you against the jutted stars
> And shout into the ridges of the wind.
> Streets coming fast,
> One after the other,
> Wedge you away from me,
> And the lamps of the city prick my eyes
> So that I can no longer see your face.
> Why should I leave you,
> To wound myself upon the sharp edges of the night?
> (*C,* 43)

"The Taxi" is a very different poem from anything in *A Dome of Many-Coloured Glass*—it shows a new sense of restraint and understatement absent even from many of the narratives in *Sword Blades and Poppy Seed.* Not having to rhyme undoubtedly helped Lowell to avoid the artificialities and wordiness of her earliest work, but she has also learned to use strong verbs—"beats," "wedge," "prick," "wound"—which express the loneliness of her separation as a physical sensation and, ultimately, a pain. Adding to this effect, the stars are

jutted, the wind has ridges, and the night is like a knife. With a
minimum of description, and none at all of the taxi, the scene ma-
terializes; objects stand out and disappear, conveying a sense of motion and accenting the speaker's emotional loss.

But Lowell has also begun to use description more effectively, by
relating it more organically to theme and giving it a strong emotional
tone. In "The Precinct, Rochester," she makes the cathedral gardens,
warm and peaceful and bordered by a Roman wall, a symbol of both
the beauty and the obsolescence of religion in modern times. In
"Clear, with Light Variable Winds," another allegory about the pursuit of unattainable beauty, the poet has a vision of a woman standing
in the fountain of his garden. Lowell was attracted to female beauty,
and her description of the woman's naked body is seductive and
precise:[10]

> Is it singing that he hears?
> A song of playing at ball?
> The moonlight shines on the straight column of water,
> And through it he sees a woman,
> Tossing the water-balls.
> Her breasts point outwards,
> And the nipples are like buds of peonies.
> Her flanks ripple as she plays,
> And the water is not more undulating
> Than the lines of her body.
>
> (C, 57–58)

Like a siren or naiad, she entices the poet to believe her, his dream,
more real and more beautiful than his "day ladies." But despite her
peony breasts, the woman is only water, and in embracing her the
poet drowns.

Lowell does not stress or call attention to the mythological associations of the water nymph, just as she does not take sides in the conflict between religious and secular values in "The Precinct, Rochester."
Rather, image, action, and setting evoke the presence of an archetypal
temptress in the one poem, and point to a clash between the need for
faith and the need for bread in the other. Lowell reduces other poems
even more severely to a single dominant image, as in "Aubade," perhaps the most imagistic poem in *Sword Blades and Poppy Seed*.

> As I would free the white almond from the green husk
> So would I strip your trappings off,
> Beloved.
> And fingering the smooth and polished kernel
> I should see that in my hands glittered a gem beyond counting.
>
> (C, 73)

Restrained, yet sensuous, "Aubade" is a distinctly erotic poem—Lowell uses the same image of an unsheathed almond as a symbol for the young male body in "White and Green," the poem immediately preceding "Aubade." Here she imaginatively touches the other's nakedness, holding in her hands the kernel or treasure of his sexuality.

In "The Bungler" Lowell returns to the fear she had voiced in "A Fairy Tale," that she would never be fulfilled by love. Now, however, instead of discoursing at length about her feelings, as she had in the early poem, she dramatizes them in a single action. As in "Aubade," her language is almost entirely pictorial—specific, uncluttered, and unforced.

> You glow in my heart
> Like the flames of uncounted candles.
> But when I go to warm my hands,
> My clumsiness overturns the light,
> And then I stumble
> Against the table and chairs.
>
> (C, 41)

The details orchestrate a fine dramatic transition from the conventional warm candle light, and the emotional presence of another, to the abrupt hard edges of the chairs and emptiness. Like "A Fairy Tale," "The Bungler" almost certainly stems from Lowell's self-consciousness about her obesity and awkwardness, but Lowell has learned to put a greater distance between the woman who feels and the artist who creates. She has achieved an objectivity even in her most personal poems, and with it has gained a greater understanding of her art. Poems like "The Taxi," "Aubade," and "The Bungler" show her to be a more sophisticated and surefooted poet than she was two years before. Within a year of *Sword Blades and Poppy Seed* she would write one of her masterpieces, "Patterns."

Lowell has not yet mastered free verse—she had only recently discovered it. Yet its liberating effects upon her language are evident, not only in the free-verse lyrics, but in some of her more conventional poems as well. As she had in *Dome,* she included sonnets in *Sword Blades and Poppy Seed.* One of them, "In Answer to a Request," is a fifteen-line sonnet that Lowell wrote to explain why she could not write a sonnet. The best features of her free verse are present here— strong verbs, crisp images, conciseness. She is putting to use in traditional poetry what she has learned from the new poetry:

> You ask me for a sonnet. Ah, my Dear,
>   Can clocks tick back to yesterday at noon?
>   Can cracked and fallen leaves recall last June
> And leap up on the boughs, now stiff and sere?
> For your sake, I would go and seek the year,
>   Faded beyond the purple ranks of dune,
>   Blown sands of drifted hours, which the moon
> Streaks with a ghostly finger, and her sneer
>   Pulls at my lengthening shadow. Yes, 'tis that!
>   My shadow stretches forward, and the ground
> Is dark in front because the light's behind.
>   It is grotesque, with such a funny hat,
>   In watching it and walking I have found
> More than enough to occupy my mind.
>
> I cannot turn, the light would make me blind.
>   (C, 43)

As a sonneteer, Lowell cannot compete with such moderns as Hopkins or Frost; even here she relies on the overused rhymes of "noon/ June/moon." But the images of cracked leaves leaping back on the boughs, of the sneering moon, and of the lengthening shadow with a funny hat give the poem conciseness and help solidify the theme of slipping, irrecoverable time. From octave to sestet, Lowell's perspective shifts from a large vista of time in the barren trees and the blown sands to her own reflection darkening in front of her—in that alone, her single exposure to time, there is "more than enough" to occupy her mind. In thematic resonance and verbal resource, "In Answer to a Request" is a considerable advance over the sonnet "To John Keats" in *Dome.* For despite what Lowell says here about seeking the year behind her, as a poet she was moving ahead—not away from the light, but toward it.

Chapter Four
Narrative Poetry I:
Lowell's Different Voices

With *Men, Women and Ghosts,* which she calls "a book of stories," Lowell emerges as an accomplished narrative poet. She had a wide-ranging sense of narrative, moreover, and in *Men, Women and Ghosts,* she "stretched" the word "stories" to include "narrative poems, properly so called; tales divided into scenes; and a few pieces of less obvious storytelling import in which one might say that the *dramatis personae* are air, clouds, trees, houses, streets, and such like things."[1] *Men, Women and Ghosts* opens with a dramatic monologue, "Patterns," and closes with "Towns in Colour," descriptive pieces written in "the unrelated method." It includes historical romances, grim New England tragedies, and war poems. A number of these, as well as some later narrative and dramatic poems, suffer from the theatricalism and overwriting that often marred Lowell's earlier work. But even excluding the poems in *Can Grande's Castle* and *Legends,* which I discuss in the following chapter, there are many more successful narratives and monologues in Lowell's middle and later books than can be dealt with here. She had the knack of storytelling. And in the years left to her after 1916—years of recurring ill health and pain, of exhausting public readings and work on the Keats book—she further perfected her narrative gifts. Her three posthumous books—*What's O'Clock, East Wind,* and *Ballads for Sale*—contain some of her very best stories and monologues.

For this chapter I have adopted the arrangement Lowell used in *Men, Women and Ghosts* to divide her narratives into four categories: poems of thwarted passion and sexual conflict—"Patterns" and its related monologues and romances; the New England stories; the "stories" told in the unrelated method; and war poems. The categories do not reflect rigid or clear-cut distinctions, for many of the New England tales also deal with frustrated passions, for instance, and "Patterns" is, at least indirectly, about war. There is unity as well as diversity in Lowell's stories. But the New England poems, which often use dialect, are readily identifiable by their setting and atmosphere, and "Patterns" has much more in common with such later poems as "Appuldurcombe Park" and "Anecdote" than it does with most of the war poems in *Men, Women and Ghosts*. Though not perfect, the classification helps to identify and locate the more persistent themes and interests among Lowell's various stories. Because the categories are not all equally important I give much more space to the New England tales and to "Patterns" and its related stories than to the other two. Aside from *Can Grande's Castle,* which needs separate consideration, and a few other exceptions, Lowell's war poems tend to be minor; and she did little with the unrelated method as a narrative technique after *Men, Women and Ghosts*. The New England poems of that book, however, lead to the powerfully told tales of *East Wind*. And "Patterns" is the first of a number of major narrative and dramatic poems dealing with the passions and the restraints between men and women.

"Patterns" and Other Relations between the Sexes

"Patterns" is almost certainly Lowell's best-known poem, as well as one of her undoubted masterpieces. First published in the August 1915 issue of the *Little Review,* it has appeared frequently in anthologies and textbooks since, and its speaker—an eighteenth-century English woman whose fiancé has just been killed fighting with the duke in Flanders—is one of the familiar characters in American poetry. Her passionate outcry against her personal loss and against such universal evils as war and artificial restraint makes her a vividly realized and timeless, tragic figure.

An expertly constructed monologue, "Patterns" contains the subtle tonal and musical effects that Lowell argued free verse was capable of. The poem is both too long and too familiar to be quoted in its entirety, but the first stanza illustrates the artistry of Lowell's word sounds, rhythm, and design:

> I walk down the garden paths,
> And all the daffodils
> Are blowing, and the bright blue squills.
> I walk down the patterned garden-paths
> In my stiff, brocaded gown.

> With my powdered hair and jewelled fan,
> I too am a rare
> Pattern. As I wander down
> The garden paths.

(C, 75)

Besides the internal and the end rhymes, assonance threads through and links the lines: w*a*lk, g*a*rden, *a*ll; p*a*ths, d*a*ffodils, p*a*tterned, f*a*n; daff*o*dils, bl*o*wing, br*o*caded; squ*i*lls, st*i*ff; g*ow*n, p*ow*dered. Alliteration occurs in "blowing . . . bright blue" and "patterned garden-paths"; and consonance or near rhyme in "gown" and "fan." Such interweaving sound patterns, of course, are appropriate in a poem about the social patterns that enmesh human life. The circular figure of the stanza—from "I walk down the garden paths" to "I wander down / The garden paths"—emphasizes the trapped, circular movement of the speaker, who will walk in her garden the rest of her life as one pacing a prison cell.

Rhythmically, "Patterns" ranks with the best free-verse poems of Lowell's era. The cadence, as well as the diction, is that of unaffected but impassioned human speech—Lowell's ideal for poetry as it had been Wordsworth's more than a hundred years earlier. Though it is the language of prose, it is cadenced, not chopped up arbitrarily but designed to fall into rhythmic units. The lines quoted are essentially iambic and have from two to four accents per line, with varying numbers of syllables. The first five lines, I believe, can be scanned as follows:

> Ĭ wălk dówn thĕ gárdĕn páths,
> Ănd áll thĕ dáffŏdĭls
> Ăře blówĭng, ănd thĕ bríght blŭe squílls.
> Ĭ wălk dówn thĕ páttĕrned gárdĕn-páths
> Ĭn m̆y stíff, brŏcádĕd gówn.

As we have seen, in her preface for *Some Imagist Poets, 1916* Lowell compared the writer of free verse to someone who had the task of walking round a circle in two minutes, his only requirement being to complete each half circle in exactly a minute. Otherwise, he is free to increase or slacken his pace, go fast or slow. In "Patterns," she balances the rapidly moving third line, with its three unstressed syllables in a row, with the slower and heavier fifth line—thus contrasting the light, breeze-blown flowers of the one with the stiff gown of the other. The jammed accents and the dead stop of the period slow the movement even more two lines later: "Í tóo aṁ ă ráre / Pátteřn." The slowing down suggests the speaker's hesitation to admit what she must about herself, while the line break is like a catch in her thought, for she is not what one might expect her to call herself— not a rare flower or thing of beauty—but a pattern walking a pattern. In thus integrating rhythm with self-discovery, accent with insight, Lowell simply demonstrates her command of the poetic craft.

But there is likeness as well as difference between the woman and the flowers she walks among. Both represent civilization's notion of beauty. The garden is nature pruned and arranged by man; the woman likewise is gorgeously arrayed and socially correct in whale-bone and brocade. Her dress makes a pink and silver stain on the edge of the garden, as if she were one of the flowers. But whereas she suffers under the restraints and stiffness of society's patterns, the flowers do not. With more freedom than she has, the flowers can flutter "in the breeze / As they please." They touch and feel the air with their bodies. The speaker's body is imprisoned, and she can release herself only in dream and wishful thinking, in which she imagines herself naked and leading her lover in a maze. She wants to be her own "pink and silver" signaling to her lover, and she would press her body, not against his naked body, but against the signs of the pattern that restrains and encases him—his sword hilt, the buttons of his waistcoat that would bruise her body as he clasped her. Her dream is to be free herself and, by exposing and opposing her flesh to his uniform, liberate him as well.[2]

In effect, she is a modern Eve who dreams of tempting her lover back to *the* garden, to a state of innocence before the fall and the necessity of the stiff clothes that conceal them from each other and the patterns that separate them. But whereas Adam awoke to find his dream of Eve to be true, her dream only taunts her.[3] For the woman's garden, the product of civilization, is already fallen and contains a serpent sent from civilization—the letters that "squirmed like snakes" on the missive informing her of her lover's death. Rather than showing her the forbidden fruit, the serpent—death—denies it to her. Yet, though she is Eve without Adam and without the chance to sin, she is penalized—not expelled from the garden as her prototype was, but forced to remain in it. In a month, she says, "We would have broken the pattern"; now, she cannot even express her emotions as she feels them:

The blue and yellow flowers stood up proudly in the sun,
Each one.
I stood upright too,
Held rigid to the pattern
By the stiffness of my gown.

(C, 76)

She will not feel the water of the fountain stroking her body like a dear hand—will not be reborn. In summer and in winter she will walk the garden paths, while the squills and daffodils "give place to pillared roses, and to asters, and to snow." In the natural pattern of generation and decay, however, the flowers and trees at least send forth their blossoms before they die. She will remain rigid and unchanging. The explosive last line—"Christ! What are patterns for?"—is thus the poignant protest of one sacrificed figure to another, a barren Eve to the second Adam.

"Appuldurcombe Park," a dramatic monologue included in the mostly lyrical *Pictures of the Floating World,* deals even more explicitly with frustrated passion and sexual needs:

I am a woman, sick for passion,
Sitting under the golden beech-trees.
I am a woman, sick for passion,
Crumbling the beech leaves to powder in my fingers.
The servants say: "Yes, my Lady," and "No, my Lady."
And all day long my husband calls me
From his invalid chair:
"Mary, Mary, where are you, Mary? I want you."
Why does he want me?
When I come, he only pats my hand
And asks me to settle his cushions.

(C, 233)

Again it is the eighteenth century and the principal setting is a garden, but the Appuldurcombe flowers are more sensuous and vibrant than those in "Patterns," while the woman's emotions rage more intensely:

Parrot flowers, toucan-feathered flowers,
How bright you are!
You hurt me with your colours,
Your reds and yellows lance at me like flames.

(C, 233)

Symbolizing the passionate needs that her invalid and presumably impotent husband cannot satisfy, the flowers both arouse her desires and threaten her with them, for she can be cured of her sickness only by adultery. Then, in an effective use of cinematic dissolve, the flashing red flowers become the scarlet coat of her "Cousin-Captain," who makes illicit love to her in the garden at night.

> Keep away from me, Cousin-Captain.
> Your scarlet coat dazzles and confuses me.
> O heart of red blood, what shall I do!
> Even the lilies blow for the bee.
>
> (C, 234)

This time the woman sins. Her heart blossoms like the sensuous toucan-colored flowers that hurt her with their loveliness, and identifies itself not with the purity of the lily, but with the passion of the rose. "Under my black dress a rose is blooming. / A rose?—a heart?—it rustles for you with open petals."

But the sinning woman meets the same sterile and unfulfilling fate as the unfallen Eve of "Patterns." The Cousin-Captain proves false and does not return when she sends for him after her husband's death. He had wanted her only for sex. "Your coat lied," she realizes. "Only your white sword spoke the truth." And she realizes too that the husband she wronged at least needed her. Stricken with guilt and now more sick than before, she imagines she hears her dead husband calling her; his voice mixes and blends with the snow that now covers all the flowers, just as winter descended on the garden in "Patterns." Betrayed by passion and the man in scarlet, still wedded in her widowhood to the cold, sterile man whom she betrayed, she apparently goes insane and prepares a "little dish of posset" for her husband, as she used to do when he was alive. "Do the dead eat?" she wonders. "I have done it so long, / So strangely long." The snow-covered tower-clock strikes eleven over the barren waste of her life—the same hour it struck when she parted from her lover in the garden to take posset to her husband. In effect, she has not moved forward; the pattern she hoped to break with her sin still controls her.

In *Men, Women and Ghosts,* "Patterns" is followed by two long narratives in rhyming, metrical stanzas that also deal with a lover's triangle similar to that of "Appuldurcombe Park." The protagonist of both is a woman sick or starved for passion. In "Pickthorn Manor," her husband, like the fiancé in "Patterns," is fighting with the duke in Flanders. In "The Cremona Violin," also set in the eighteenth century, the protagonist's husband is a devoted concert violinist. In both, an ardent, illicit lover steps into the place vacated by the absent or preoccupied husband, tempting the women and throwing them into an internal conflict between their strong sense of marital duty and their desire for a passionate relationship. Passion prevails; but because the women love their unresponsive husbands more than they do the illicit lovers, their passion is also frustrated.

In "Pickthorn Manor," the newly married Lady Eunice waits for the return of her husband, Sir Everard Frampton, from the Flanders war. One day in early spring she comes upon a young man, Gervase Deane, fishing in Sir Everard's stream. Gervase has been sent home wounded from Flanders, and because he can tell her many stories of Sir Everard's valor, Eunice befriends him and the two meet often. Gervase is soon in love, however, and begins to read poetry to Eunice to express his feelings without openly declaring them. Although Eunice remains faithful to her husband, the afternoons with Gervase by the river, under the budding leaves, are the happiest she has had in a long time. In effect, Gervase is arousing feelings in her that she can only have for Sir Everard, and unconsciously she is beginning to confuse the two. One day, as Gervase is shaking ripe cherries to her from a tree, Eunice stumbles over a rake and stuns herself. Having desired her husband for so long, when she awakes she imagines that it is he bending over her, whereas in fact it is Gervase. She calls him her love, which Gervase naturally interprets as an admission of her feelings for him. He kisses her passionately, and "all her glowing / Youth answered him" (C, 82), but as they embrace, an old retainer of Sir Everard's spots them. Only when Gervase threatens the man does Eunice recognize him as Gervase. But she is still under the delusion that Everard has returned, and demands that Gervase leave her and her husband alone. Her passion, stirred and enflamed by Gervase, yet repressed and always associated in her mind with her husband, has deranged her mind. When Gervase explains her mistake to her, Eunice does not leave her room for days—afraid "Of what her eyes might trick her into seeing, / Of what her longing urge her then to do"—though she is "tortured" and made ill by her solitude (C, 83). Out of pity for Gervase, she agrees to meet him during the summer, but only as brother and sister, and their talk is stiff and without pleasure for either.

Finally, Sir Everard returns in the fall and comes upon Eunice when she is expecting to meet Gervase. The earlier delusion repeats itself, only now Eunice sees Sir Everard as Gervase, the illicit lover. She tries to flee, and when her husband catches her, her senses blur; her gaze is "hunted" and "fearful," and she keeps calling Everard Gervase (C, 85). She has totally confused the two men: the lover who stayed with her and shared her days like a husband, the husband who now chases her through the trees like a lover. Having fought against her feelings and needs for so long, she cannot at first recognize that she is now free to express them. Everard expects her to respond as if the long waiting had made no difference. But as he puts his hand on her breast and tries to kiss her,

> She started
> As one sharp lashed with whips,
> And pushed him from her, moaning, his dumb quest
> Denied and shuddered from.
>
> (C, 85)

Subconsciously, she is rejecting Everard as her husband, punishing him for deserting her, just as earlier her sexual needs responded to Gervase, whom she turned into the husband she longed for. This time, Eunice rejoices when she discovers her error, but Everard has returned too late. In mistaking him for Gervase, Eunice reveals how much Gervase has replaced him. In fact, she cannot resist Gervase's appeal to meet him one last time at the river. Everard has learned from his old retainer about the scene under the cherry tree, and thinking that his wife is unfaithful, he follows her. As Eunice and Gervase are pushing off in a boat to be out of earshot, Everard jumps on them, and he and Eunice drown.

Eunice is thus a victim of her own passion, which drew her to Gervase; of her innocence and strong sense of duty and marital love, which kept Everard's image constantly before her; and of the inability of the two men to comprehend her. With her husband in Flanders, she is a woman in love, but without an approved outlet for her love. To deny herself the meetings with Gervase would mean isolation and loneliness in the manor. Yet as the meetings continue, the stand-in for her husband becomes, in effect, her natural husband—a fertility figure associated with the budding spring, trees, abundant fruit, the river and fish. Emotionally bereft, waiting through a barren period, Eunice cannot resist the passion that Gervase arouses, yet her attachment to Everard will not allow her consciously to accept Gervase as a lover. Passion and fidelity join when Eunice knows Everard has returned, but now Everard casts her into the conflicting roles of wife and lover. Forbidden any meeting with Gervase, Eunice suffers more emotional pain and loneliness from her husband's suspicions and coldness than when Everard was absent. At last, the Edenic garden of the manor changes into a winter wasteland, and the river of life where Eunice first met Gervase becomes the waters of death where she and Everard drown.[4]

Very much like a character in one of Hardy's novels, Eunice is destroyed by the conflicting patterns of nature—her sexual needs—society, and her own personality. Charlotta Altgelt, the heroine of "The Cremona Violin," is caught in a similar predicament, although she is not as passive or innocent as Eunice, and ultimately revolts against her husband.

Charlotta also loves her husband deeply, but Theodore Altgelt, a master violinist, loves his violin "Above all things" (C, 89). He devotes his life to his art—to rehearsals, concerts, and the care of his instrument. Charlotta resents his neglect, and in the first part of the poem she pleads with him to spend the evening with her. But Altgelt does not recognize her feelings, and goes off to the concert hall:

> Now she sat
> Alone again, always alone, the trend
> Of all her thinking brought her back to that
> She wished to banish. What would life be? What?
> For she was young, and loved, while he was moved
> Only by music.
>
> (C, 90)

On the other hand, Charlotta is moved by Altgelt's music too, and she loves him because of what he can do with his instrument. She even longs to be the violin from which he can produce such beautiful sounds:

> Had he but guessed she was another one,
> Another violin. Her strings were aching,
> Stretched to the touch of his bow hand, again
> He played and she almost broke at the strain.
>
> (C, 90)

In fact, she is moved far more passionately by the music than Altgelt is. While he is concerned with the technical details of a new

score, or the mechanics to be gotten through before and during a performance, the music transports her to a vibrant, dreamlike world.
When she is allowed to attend one of his performances, Altgelt's music obliterates everything from her mind but itself and the two of
them.

> The first notes from the orchestra sent skimming
> Her outward consciousness. Her brain was fused
> Into the music, Theodore's music! Used
> To hear him play, she caught his single tone.
> For all she noticed they two were alone.
>
> (C, 97)

She is at her most passionate and is most alive when Altgelt is playing, the music stimulating her to an emotional climax that is like a
sexual orgasm. But afterward, she cannot express or make him understand what she felt. He is only concerned with "How this thing
had gone well, that badly" (C, 97), and when they reach home, he
attends first to his instrument, to see if the evening air has affected
its wood. Only when Charlotta flings herself against him, desperately
insisting on his love, does Altgelt become aware of her feelings and
recognize that he must be "made of wood" (C, 98).

But by now—part 4 of the poem—Charlotta has had an affair with
another man. Her conscience bothers her, though she tries to convince herself that Altgelt is still her lover, and not the other—one
Heinrich Marohl, whom she met on the night she begged Altgelt to
remain home instead of going to the concert hall. When they meet
again, in part 2 of the poem, it is by prearrangement. Like Eunice,
Charlotta becomes involved with another man because she cannot express her feelings to the husband she loves. But unlike Eunice, Charlotta admits the sexual attraction between her and Heinrich, who
does not conceal his feelings as Gervase did: "Frau Altgelt knew she
toyed with fire, knew / That what her husband lit this other man /
Fanned to hot flame" (C, 95). She tells herself that she "ran / No
danger since she knew what things to ban" (C, 95), but she cannot
keep from compromising herself. Heinrich has insisted on buying her
a locket and chain. After he has put it on her neck, Charlotta suddenly felt "as though a strain / Were put upon her, collared like a
slave, / Leashed in the meshes of this thing he gave" (C, 95). She is
in the trap of passion, and although she tries to take the chain off,
she cannot unsnap or break it. Altgelt, innocent and unsuspecting

because fundamentally ignorant of the depth and strength of his wife's feelings, even after she has made him acknowledge her, assumes that the locket is a present from her mother and insists that she wear it where it can be seen.

It was, of course, her fear of committing sin with Heinrich to satisfy her needs that led to Charlotta's passionate confrontation with her husband. After that, she resolves to see Heinrich no more, and for a time her marriage is happy. She even "found her husband all that she had felt / His music to contain" (*C,* 99). And she takes pleasure in her commonplace domestic tasks and routine. But her content within such limitations lasts only so long as Altgelt is an attentive husband. When he becomes absorbed in the preparations for a new opera by Mozart and begins to neglect her again, her thoughts return to Heinrich. She still wears his locket, which, rather than the collar of a slave, now "seemed to her a bit / Of some gone youth" (*C,* 100); and in a confusion of identities similar to that of "Pickthorn Manor," she hears Heinrich's voice in the notes played by Altgelt. Soon she and Heinrich are meeting again, and caught between her impulse to yield to Heinrich's urging that they run away and the power that her husband's music still has over her, she sometimes "wished to kill / Herself to solve her problem" (*C,* 100).

Thus, the artist, devoted to spiritual pursuits, produces emotions in his wife that his total dedication to art causes him to neglect, so that Charlotta, sensuously aroused by her husband's music, turns and becomes vulnerable to a purely physical man, which her husband cannot be. The violin, which could lift Charlotta to moments of perfect union with Altgelt, is also a barrier between them, and ultimately she hates it as a rival. Fingering the lock and chain, which she received from a man who regarded her as a woman, she rejects Altgelt, smashes his fine Stradivarius on the floor, and leaves her home.

As long narratives, both "Pickthorn Manor" and "The Cremona Violin" depend much more on psychological insight and internal conflict than, say, the long adventure of Max Breuck in *Sword Blades and Poppy Seed.* Whereas that poem made extensive use of physical description, the action of these is composed largely of the emotions and thoughts of Eunice and Charlotta. Lowell probes their conscious and unconscious selves to explore the frustrations and needs of women who are emotionally starved by the husbands they love. Having to wait alone, or confined to a strictly domestic role, both attract the physical lovers they need to fulfill their lives, yet it is not sexuality without love that they seek, but a union of the two in the husband as a passionate lover. Failing to understand their wives and excluding them from the activities in which they are most involved, Everard and Altgelt bring destruction on their marriages. Their passions—for war and the management of Pickthorn, for music—are essentially asexual and at odds with the strong passionate natures of their wives. Though Everard becomes a suspicious, watchful husband of a woman who has struggled to remain faithful to him, and Altgelt remains almost childishly unconcerned about his wife, who is wearing her lover's gift around her throat, Eunice and Charlotta feel a similar guilt and resentment. Both poems, in effect, portray the suffering and the sexual divisions that result from the man's inability to perceive what is essential to the woman who is dependent upon him.[5]

Division and conflict between the sexes is the explicit theme and organizing principle of one of Lowell's last poems, "Anecdote," published in the posthumous *Ballads for Sale*. "Anecdote" is composed of two soliloquies, the first of which is a man's.

> Her breasts were small, upright, virginal;
> Even through her clothes I could feel the nipples pointing
>   upward when I touched her inadvertently.
> The chastity of her garments was pronounced,
> But no disposal of material could keep the shape of her
>   breasts unseen.
>
> (C, 576)

The man perceives what he is attracted to in the woman—her sensuous body beneath a chaste exterior. He is so conscious of her breasts that he can feel her nipples through her clothes, even when he touches her inadvertently. They are, apparently, more than friends. Yet she is teasing him, he believes, and unnaturally withholding herself from him, as if determined not to let the passions she has aroused in him ruffle her passionless demeanor. She walks and behaves as if she were superior to the sexual desire that she must know is tormenting him. Angry at the distant airs of a woman whom he has already possessed in his imagination and who dominates over his thoughts, he wants her to acknowledge him as her lover.

The woman's soliloquy is somewhat longer; not surprisingly, it gives a different picture of their relationship. For the woman, the man's lovemaking is like a "dagger tipped with honey." He has "parted" her from herself. And rather than feeling secure within a correct virginal exterior, she feels as if she has been stripped of her clothes; the man has exposed her.

> I caught my garments about me,
> But they withered one by one as leaves wither, and fell.
> I was alone in the wide sunlight;
> His eyes were winds which would not leave me.
>
> (*C,* 577)

The love, which her imagery shows she has acknowledged, has left her defenseless and vulnerable. But if it shames her to reveal her feelings, she also rejoices at the chance to express them. As with the speaker in "Patterns," love would free her from restraint, parting her passionate self from the socially correct roles she admits she is well trained in. But now she finds that the man is distant and unresponsive. He does not see that she is aroused by him and that it is "agony" to hold herself apart from him. What he thought to be her respectable, frosty demeanor is a "strain" that is "choking" her—can he not see through her "pretense," she wonders. While she is ready to break the patterns that keep them apart and can barely conceal her sexual feelings, he does nothing but talk or intellectualize, and she realizes that he does not want a confrontation with passion. He has exposed her "for a whim," but is "as impassive as a stone Hermes before whom Venus herself would need no cloak" (*C,* 577). He was attracted to her breasts when they were modestly covered, and turns away from the woman who feels naked. She was sexually interesting to him, apparently, only while she kept her passions hidden in a virginal dress.

"Anecdote," however, does not allow us to pass final judgment on the man, any more than on the woman, because it does not clearly endorse one view as more correct or true than the other. Each of them wants a sexual relation with the other, but each experiences in the other a fear of or retreat from sexuality. The reader is allowed to see both speakers from two perspectives—the image each speaker has of himself or herself, and the image each presents to the other—but the man and the woman know each other only as he or she perceives the other. Thus sexual division, their ignorance of each other, is one of the dominant impressions left by the poem. Isolated in separate soliloquies, in one of Lowell's most convincing poems of frustrated passion, the speakers talk only to themselves without communicating.

"New Heavens for Old," also from *Ballads for Sale,* presents a radical reworking of the theme of "Patterns." The speaker sits indoors, feeling the uselessness of her life and looking at an almanac of the year when she was born—she has done nothing with her time. Outside, her "fellows" shout for her to join them. They are vibrant,

"fresh," and "indecent"; and they fill the street with their exuberant
physical energy.

> Young men with naked hearts jeering between iron house-fronts,
> Young men with naked bodies beneath their clothes
> Passionately conscious of them,
> Ready to strip off their clothes,
> Ready to strip off their customs, their usual routine,
> Clamouring for the rawness of life,
> In love with appetite,
> Proclaiming it as a creed,
> Worshipping youth,
> Worshipping themselves.
>
> (C, 574)

In the preceding poems about the sexes, we have seen the woman's
passion having to contend with social restraints and with the frustrations caused by an absent or imperceptive male. "New Heavens for
Old" celebrates the sexual vitality and freedom of the man. As they
"bare . . . their lusts," the young men become a raw masculine
force, roaring and exploding upon the "dead houses like new, sharp
fire." Unashamed of their instincts, but rather Whitmanesque in
their love of their bodies and acceptance of physical appetites, "They
call for women and the women come" (C, 574).

The speaker, however, remains in her room, a lonely voyeur. The
scene and her situation are almost certainly derived from section 11
of Whitman's "Song of Myself." Whitman describes a lonely woman
looking through the windows of her house at twenty-eight young
men bathing by the shore. As in Lowell, the sensual exuberance and
freedom of the men contrasts with the barren, sheltered life of the
woman. But in Whitman, the woman imaginatively joins the men to
become the twenty-ninth bather and their unseen lover, passing her
invisible hand over their bodies and seizing fast to them without their
knowing it. Lowell's speaker, though drawn to the masculine energy
she so forcefully describes, holds back even from imaginative partici-
pation in it. The spectacle astonishes and excites her, and of course
it is because she has suppressed her own instincts that she sees the
men in strong sexual terms. But when they call for women, and "bare
the whiteness of their lusts" to the house she gazes from, she resists
and instead of joining them arranges three roses in a Chinese vase:

A pink one,
A red one,
A yellow one.
I fuss over their arrangement.
Then I sit in a South window
And sip pale wine with a touch of hemlock in it,
And think of Winter nights,
And field-mice crossing and re-crossing
The spot which will be my grave.

(C, 574)

She turns from the passion displayed in the streets to a life of patterns, arranging and fussing over the flowers that will die in their vase, just as she endures, or has chosen, a living death in her room. She mixes poison with her wine and thinks of winter. Having held herself back from passion, she is mentally in the sterile, dead world that descended on the passionate, struggling women of "Patterns," "Appuldurcombe Park," and "Pickthorn Manor." But whereas they reached for and were denied a "new heaven," she denies it to herself—not, however, without a sense of regret and a tragic self-awareness of her desolation as strong as in any of those who gambled and lost. In fact, what Lowell suggests in these poems is the tragedy of "Patterns" repeating itself and becoming more harrowing and more difficult to overcome, as the patterns, the system of customs and restraints, become more and more internalized.

The New England Tales

Lowell's presentation of life in rural New England is even more harrowing and stark. She greatly admired Frost's *North of Boston* because it portrayed the physical and emotional depletion of a people whose native vigor, she believed, had been drained by war and emigration. And her New England is perhaps more desolate than Frost's in that it is mostly unrelieved by the courage and endurance that Frost found among its people. In the four New England poems published in *Men, Women and Ghosts* as "The Overgrown Pasture," and in the later New England poems collected in the posthumous *East Wind*, Lowell's characters are lonely, hopeless figures, often driven to despair, violence, or suicidal acts. Their lives have become unstrung, meaningless, desperate; many of them live in or near decaying, ruined houses that match their lives. Superstition and supernatural events occur in a number of the stories, which become tales of horror, mystery, the unknown. Lowell's rural New England is a broken country, a ruined garden, half real and half ghostly, caught between decaying or dead traditions and an empty present.

Loneliness is a dominant theme, especially in "The Overgrown Pasture" poems, which include three monologues by women who, speaking in dialect, present New England versions of the "Patterns" tragedy of passion frustrated or denied. "Reaping" is a wife's confession to her husband that she has been unfaithful; she also reminds him how strong her love was when they married.

> When I married yer I loved yer.
> Why, your voice 'ud make
> Me go hot and cold all over,
> An' your kisses most stopped my heart from beatin'.
>
> (C, 130)

But she is quickly disillusioned. Their marriage fails because, as she admits, she became a "mopey wife" after the death of their only child, and because her husband "was all took up with the farm." Spending much of her time alone, she longs for him to notice her, for any kind of contact with him, even at secondhand.

> I'd foller yer around like a dog,
> An' set in the chair you'd be'n settin' in,
> Jest to feel its arms around me,
> So long's I didn't have yours.
>
> (C, 130)

But her husband pays so little attention to her he did not notice that another man, Elmer, was "hangin' around" the farm the previous winter. He leaves his wife alone with Elmer, who is supposed to fix the phone, while he goes off for the day. Elmer fixes the phone in minutes, then stays for dinner and helps the woman with the dishes. Elmer wants the woman sexually, and though she "fended him off" at first, "He got all he wanted":

> An' I give it to him,
> An' what's more, I'm glad!
> I ain't dead, anyway,
> An' somebody thinks I'm somethin'.
>
> (C, 131)

Violating her own deeply held laws in a desperate attempt for love, and to be something to somebody, she finds herself deserted by her lover—Elmer has not been back for two months—and now sexually attractive to her husband. He responds to her confession by attempting to make love to her—probably to reclaim his possession of her. But it is too late, and she resists him: "It" wouldn't be "decent." Having divided the roles of wife and lover, having been denied for so long the chance to be both, she now can be neither.

In "Off the Turnpike," the speaker is a widow who has lived in mental terror for eight years. Six months after her husband's death, she came upon a man's hand in some laylock bushes by the side of her house. Thinking that a drunken tramp had fallen asleep in her laylocks, she tried to pull him to the barn, only to find there was no body attached to the hand. She cannot find any sign of the body and finally buries the hand. Years later, when she had grown used to the thought of "that awful night" (C, 133), she decides to dig up the hand, just to be certain that it had been flesh and bone and not a figment of her imagination. Now there is no sign of the hand—no bones, not even the ring she had noticed on its little finger. Worried about her sanity, afraid to tell anyone about the hand because she might be committed to an asylum, she digs for months in a frantic search until her hired boy catches her at it. Now she has sold the farm and is going to live in Chicago—far enough away to keep her from ever coming back.

We do not know, in fact, if the woman is insane, or if her country has been playing a cruel joke on her by inexplicably revealing the hand and making her question her sanity, and then hiding from her the only proof that she is not insane. Possibly Lowell knew of the numerous myths in which dismemberment is associated with fertility, and used this dismembered hand to controvert the myth.[6] For rather than experiencing renewal or rebirth, the woman's life becomes more deranged, more barren and less social than it was before. Rather than feeling a oneness with the ground she has lived on, she feels oppressed by it, in conflict with it. Her connection with the land has disappeared as totally as the ghastly hand, and she has sold her farm to someone who "wouldn't be so stuck on the view / Ef he'd seed it every mornin' and night for forty year" as she has (C, 131). However, she cannot truly escape the land any more than she can leave behind the memories of that awful night. The "view" is "so pressed" into her that she can see it with her eyes shut.

The speaker in "Number 3 on the Docket" experiences the countryside even more as a hostile force. The forest seems to swallow her
husband when he goes into it, and it advances menacingly upon her:

> . . . I'd watch him from the kitchen winder.
> It seemed the woods come marchin' out to meet him
> An' the trees 'ud press round him an' hustle him.
> I got so I was scared o' th' trees.
> I thought they come nearer,
> Every day a little nearer,
> Closin' up round the house.
>
> (C, 137)

She especially fears and hates the winter, when snow covers everything with a dreadful monotony until it doesn't seem white any
more, but "black as ink." Worst of all, her isolation results in a life
of almost total silence. Her husband, even when he was with her,
"never spoke 'cept when he had to," and then he would only say
"yes" or "no" (C, 136). Extremely taciturn, he never perceives his
wife's need to hear the sound of a human voice. They have no phone,
no contact with the outside world, and the silence of her life becomes
so oppressive the woman begins to hear it whispering in her ears.
"Many's the time" she dropped a pan on the floor, "Jest to hear it
clatter" (C, 137). Finally driven insane, she murders her husband,
who has been like a dead man to her for much of their marriage.

> It didn't seem's though that was Ed,
> An' it didn't seem as though I was me.
> I had to break a way out somehow,
> Somethin' was closin' in
> An' I was stiflin'.
> Ed's loggin' axe was ther,
> An' I took it.
>
> (C, 138)

As in "Off the Turnpike," however, there is no "way out." Having
been a virtual prisoner most of her life, the woman is captured running through the snow in just her housedress.

Fear of the land becomes a severe form of paranoia in "The Note-
Book in the Gate-Legged Table," one of the narratives in *East Wind*.
The notebook, a diary, was written in 1889 by a mental patient sent

to an isolated farm in the Berkshires to recover his health. Instead he completely breaks down because in the countryside he is surrounded by the very thing that torments him most—the grass. He sees the grass as a pitiless, unstoppable force, almost consciously antagonistic to man and eager to devour all things human. As the terrible silence did to the woman in "Number 3 on the Docket," the grass speaks to him:

> I hear it in the night crying for men
> To feed its vitals with their own. I see
> It crawling toward this thin, unstable house,
> Thrusting its clutching fingers through the boards,
> Swallowing the poor weak flowers in their beds. . . .
>
> (C, 500)

The mad diarist's melodramatic and violent language, which reinforces the impression of his insanity, also creates a vivid, surrealistic image of nature.

As we have seen, moreover, the sense of being besieged by the landscape, of man in conflict with nature, is only somewhat more pronounced in this poem than in the others, where it also contributes to the desolation of rural life in New England. Having dealt with a land that contradicts the myth of renewal in "Off the Turnpike," Lowell evokes and revises one of the most familiar symbols of renewal and hope in American poetry—Whitman's leaves of grass. Whitman, in fact, speaks of a "spear" of grass, as the diarist accuses some of doing. The grass seems to Whitman "the beautiful uncut hair of graves"; and it is like many tongues reaching out from the mouths of the dead, speaking in a language he wishes he could translate.[7] Instead of Whitman's promise of rebirth and victory over death, the diarist sees the grass as threatening total annihilation; to be buried in it is to be consumed by a hostile nature. His hopes rise when he learns of a former resident of the farm who suffered from the same fear as his, and who arranged to have his coffin strapped under the roof of the barn and thus cheat the grass. But when he goes to admire the coffin, he discovers that it crumbled away years ago and the corpse has disappeared. Believing there is "no safety anywhere at all / For any people" (C, 502), the diarist commits suicide.

Years later, his notebook is found in the drawer of a gate-legged table purchased by a doctor. The table is one of many items being auctioned at an old farmhouse, and the doctor buys it out of pity for the abandonment suggested by the scene: "The old stock ended—it was the usual story— / Gone West, or dead, no one to keep the farm" (C, 500). Now Virginia creepers cover the porch so thickly the "lattice laths might have been creeper-stems" (C, 500). In effect, the diarist was prophetic as well as mad. Nature has successfully besieged the house and is devouring it.

An abandoned house also figures prominently in a very different story, "The Rosebud Wall-Paper." Told by a minor character, it recounts the life of Amos Sears, who lived for seventeen years with a common-law wife, after his legal wife deserted him to become a stewardess in a Halifax steamboat. Although the townspeople gossip about Amos living in sin with Mrs. Richards, whom he calls his housekeeper, the two are generally tolerated and apparently live happily until Mrs. Richards's death. The doctor, who arrives too late to save Mrs. Richards, tries in vain to comfort Amos. The two men are trapped by a snowstorm for three nights and two days, during which time Amos never leaves his post of standing rigidly by Mrs. Richards's bed. When help finally arrives from the town, he collapses. After a severe illness, Amos visits his one friend, Luke, a stonecutter, to ask him to make a gravestone for Mrs. Richards. Amos has written an inscription for the stone, declaring his love of her and proclaiming her his wife in the eyes of God. The orthodox Luke thinks it is sinful to ask God's blessing on an unsanctified union, and carves on the stone only a simple memorial: "Here lies Mary Richards. God's will be done" (C, 509). Later, however, when visiting the grave, the narrator finds Amos's original inscription scrawled in red chalk over and between Luke's lines. Knowing that Amos must be suffering intense grief, the narrator rushes to Amos's house, where he finds the living room walls covered with chalk drawings of shipwrecks—the most direful and chilling images of death at sea. They are Amos's attempts to conjure the sea to kill his runaway wife. Frightened and angry, the narrator yells at Amos, "God in Heaven, man, don't you know she was drowned in a wreck two year ago!" (C, 511). Having agreed to a separation, Amos was unable to get a divorce, and he now learns that he was free to marry Mrs. Richards before she died. In a rage, he chases the narrator out of the house, and then disappears. Six years have passed without a sign of Amos. The town, deeply disturbed by his pictures, has covered them with rosebud paper. The house, however, is falling in much faster than expected, and the narrator takes it as a symbol of Amos's life, which was "jerrybuilt" like the house.

The longest poem in *East Wind*, "The Rosebud Wall-Paper" is a powerful story because of the complexity of Amos Sears. He is not understood by the townspeople; even the narrator, who grew up with Amos, realizes that he is just beginning to know him when Amos explains the purpose of his drawings. There is little communication between Amos and the others, except for Luke, and thus Amos and Mrs. Richards can live together undisturbed. The town knows of the death of his wife for two years before Amos learns of it. When his wife left him, Amos did not seek the support of the townspeople, and he appears to them to be listless and gloomy, a man who is just hanging on. Actually, Amos is a man of strong passions, a rebel who is indifferent to the opinions of the town because he lives by his own laws. The doctor cannot fathom the depth of feeling that enables or compels Amos to stand for days and nights like a "granite boulder" over Mrs. Richards's corpse (*C*, 508)—an uncommon grief that resembles Heathcliff's in *Wuthering Heights*.[8] The strength of his love is too much even for his friend, Luke, who reduces Amos's heart-wrung prayer into a conventional phrase. When Amos's love turns to an equally strong hate, the town covers his expression of it with the rosebud paper. Just as he claimed that Mrs. Richards was God's gift to him to lighten his sorrow, and that their love was like the burning bush or revelation of God to him, so in his pictures he asserts a godlike power to command the sea. He is insane, a "jerrybuilt" man, to think he has this power, but he is also larger than life, a "granite boulder" in a town that spends its days in gossip and ordinary affairs.

The townspeople, on the other hand, such as the doctor, the parson, and the narrator, attempt to help Amos, while he isolates himself and tries to become a sorcerer. Unlike the other lonely New Englanders we have seen, Amos's solitude causes him to find powers in himself he did not know he possessed—his ability to draw. Believing that he can control nature with his art, he is, without knowing it, imitating Prospero; but whereas Prospero's magic brings reconciliation, Amos turns his creative power to destructive purposes. He cannot control nature, moreover; the death that he wants to cause has already occurred. As happens often in these stories, a character's internal world of passion and frustration replaces the external world, so that the character cannot perceive the difference between inner and outer realities. Like the woman who found the disembodied hand, or the man who feared the grass, Amos is limited to the world of his perceptions. And although he is one of the most successful of these

characters in having lived a passionate life with Mrs. Richards, he is
also one of the most thwarted. For he was free without knowing that
he was, and in plotting against a wife who is alive only in his mind
and who, in effect, has deserted him a second time, he becomes a
victim of what Thomas Hardy would call one of life's little ironies.

Similar portraits of desperate and deranged people appear throughout the *East Wind* poems. In "A Dracula of the Hills," a dying
woman uses the charms of a witch to keep her heart alive, feeding
upon the life of her husband, even after her body has been buried.
Her coffin is dug up and her heart is burned. In "The Day That Was
That Day," one woman stops another from poisoning herself—the
would-be suicide can no longer bear the emptiness and sterility of her
life. But perhaps the finest poem in the volume, "The Doll," is told
by a concert musician who has escaped the rural country and only
visits it for vacation. She does not speak in dialect; the lines are blank
verse and re-create the atmosphere of the small town of South Norton
through specific detail. With their exquisite, carefully tended, an-
tique furniture and artifacts, the homes are like museums, shutting
out the light of the present and preserving the past when South Norton was a trading village and sent its ships to China and Ceylon. But
now South Norton no longer turns to the sea; its people live in the
past without the vitality and expansiveness that characterized it. The
speaker, emancipated from such an enclosed life, is amused and
touched by the town, but returns to the city with a sense of relief
and thanks God she has read Freud (*C,* 482).

She always visits the Misses Perkins, two elderly sisters who "were
a whiff / Of eighteen-forty" (*C,* 482), and who live in one of the mu-
seumlike houses that have become mausoleums. The elder sister is
bedridden, and the younger conducts the speaker to the invalid's
room for small talk and a glass of sherry. Sitting in an armchair facing the room, however, is a large wax doll, "dressed in the Paris fashion / Of sixty years ago" (*C,* 482), which the speaker dismisses at
first as having been found in the attic during a cleaning. But each
year the doll is still there, and the speaker begins to dread

> Encountering her, she seemed so full of tales,
> Tell-tales of maiden ladies left alone
> With still things on the walls and mantlepieces
> And nothing moving round them but the sea
> Kept out of reach beyond the matted entry.
>
> (*C,* 483)

Her last visit is to offer condolence to the younger sister. But though Jane Perkins has died, Julia Perkins takes the speaker to the old room because she cannot bear to be any place else. Everything is the same, except that the bed is empty and the doll's chair has been moved to a window facing the street. Assuming that the chair is empty, but not knowing exactly why she went up to it, the speaker is startled and "may have jumped" at finding the doll still in it. "It was so dull for her after Jane died," Julia explains, "I moved her here where she could see the street" (*C*, 484). After returning that evening to Boston, the speaker stays up half the night playing Stravinsky. "I dreamt wax doll for three weeks afterwards," she admits, "And I shall go to London this vacation" (*C*, 484).

The doll of course symbolizes the death-in-life of the Misses Perkins, who have sat passively like dolls while life passed them by. They are shut-ins who have not changed over the years, like the woman in "New Heavens for Old," but no exuberant masculine force disturbs the emptiness of their street. The speaker who always found "a narrow odd contentment" in the town (*C*, 481), and who thought that she knew it, not only with the intimacy of one who grew up in it but with the wider knowledge of one who has adapted to the outside world, learns that not even Freud had enabled her to see that Julia was insane. The passion for life is so stilled in Julia that she talks to dolls as if there were no difference between living and unliving. Earlier, the speaker had wondered what would become of the house and its treasures after Julia's death; then she felt annoyed that Julia kept to her old ways even though there was no Jane to wait upon. At the end, *she* feels threatened because she can no longer trust her perceptions or her assumptions about reality, and because, in Julia's world, where dolls are equal to humans, she is reduced to the level of a doll. She has to prove she belongs to the modern world, and not to her native town, by playing Stravinsky; yet she is haunted by the doll and not confident enough of her emancipation to risk returning to South Norton. The speaker's mind, that is, becomes defensive when it recognizes the implications of insanity in another.

"The Doll" is a powerful poem—understated, suggestive, and disturbing. Most of the *East Wind* poems, in fact, are well-told stories about conflicts between men and women, people and their land, past and present; they vividly portray a place, its residents, and their problems. The best of the tales grip and keep the attention. And though most are finely crafted, Lowell's emphasis is on story rather than technique or style, which tends to be straightforward and unadorned, as in country tales in the oral tradition. By *East Wind*, Lowell was confident enough of her narrative art to keep her presence as artificer as unobtrusive as possible; and by not striving for originality, even basing many of the poems on old New England legends and newspaper accounts, she produced a work of considerable originality.[9]

Narratives in the Unrelated Method

Technique, rather than the tale, predominates in those poems written in the unrelated method that Lowell included among the narratives of *Men, Women and Ghosts*, principally "Spring Day" and "Towns in Colour." As we saw in chapter 2, Lowell learned the unrelated method from John Gould Fletcher; she experimented with it, she said, as a way of rendering "the colour, and light, and shade, of certain places and hours, stressing the purely pictorial effect, and with little or no reference to any other aspect of the places described."[10] That Lowell included in a "book of stories" poems of pure sense impression, whose *"dramatis personae* are air, clouds . . . streets, and such like things," indicates how little concerned she was with the formal definitions of genre, as opposed to finding new narrative techniques.[11] On the other hand, stories in which the chief incidents are the poet's experiences of sound and color, without much attention to plot, conflict, or character development, tend to be trivial and thin as narratives—a risk Lowell was not sufficiently aware of or was willing to take. "Spring Day," in polyphonic prose, is little more than a series of sensory details that mark morning, noon, and night. If there is a high point or climax, it is almost certainly the following passage, describing "Midday and Afternoon":

Swirl of crowded streets. Shock and recoil of traffic. The stock-still brick facade of an old church, against which the waves of people lurch and withdraw. Flare of sunshine down side-streets. Eddies of light in the window of chemists' shops, with their blue, gold, purple jars, darting colours far into the crowd. Loud bangs and tremors, murmurings out of high windows, whirring of machine belts, blurring of horses and motors. A quick spin and shudder of brakes on an electric car, and the jar of a church-bell knocking against the metal blue of the sky. I am a piece of the town, a bit of blown dust, thrust along with the crowd. (*C,* 146)

Having begun with the fragile, checkered effects of sunlight upon water in the section called "Bath," "Spring Day" uses a crescendolike development to reach this explosion of sounds and colors in the crowded streets. But the polyphonic prose, despite its deployment of rhythms and word sounds, here reads more like the notebook entry of an idea for a poem than it does a poem that tells a story, however obliquely. The language itself is sometimes unoriginal and sensorially imprecise or vague: "waves of people," "Flare of sunshine," "Loud bangs and tremors."

"Towns in Colour" is a better poem, though it is even more loosely organized as a narrative. Made up of five scenes or sensory encounters, the first four sections center on specific colors: red, white, gold, and black and grey. The fifth part, "An Aquarium," is polychromatic. Lowell is more successful here in turning objects into actors and in rendering the sensory experience of them as a narrative event. Red slippers, for instance, festoon from the ceiling, "jamming their crimson reflections against the windows of cabs and tramcars." They "balance upon arched insteps" and "swing up over curved heels like whirling tanagers" (*C*, 149)—or like the dancers they both suggest and take the place of. In "Thompson's Lunch Room," the second section, and a "Study in Whites,"

> The chalk-white spot of a cook's cap
> Moves unglossily against the vaguely bright wall—
> Dull chalk-white striking the retina like a blow
> Through the wavering uncertainty of steam.
>
> (*C*, 149)

The cook's cap replaces the cook—it moves and impresses a distinct identity in the swirl of lights and steam. Lowell is now drawing more surely upon synesthesia to combine the senses, visual and tactile in this case, so that the chalk-white strikes. In the third section, "An Opera House," the color of gold becomes something felt and heard as well as seen:

> Gold carving edges the balconies,
> Rims the boxes,
> Runs up and down fluted pillars.
> Little knife-stabs of gold
> Shine out whenever a box door is opened.
> Gold clusters
> Flash in soft explosions
> On the blue darkness,
> Suck back to a point,
> And disappear.
>
> (*C*, 150)

Gold suffuses the senses to become the thing experienced and the
medium through which it is experienced.

Lowell combines the senses brilliantly in the following lines from
the fourth section, "Afternoon Rain in State Street":

> A horse steps in a puddle,
> And white, glaring water spurts up
> In stiff, outflaring lines,
> Like the rattling stems of reeds.
>
> (C, 151)

The artisan or poet is very much in evidence here, turning a color
into a stiff tactile impression and then into a sound, which material-
izes the white lines of water into stems of reeds. The four lines are
virtually a self-contained lyric, and in fact the objectivity, precision,
and detail of the unrelated method appear more often and usually
with better effect in Lowell's shorter imagistic lyrics than in her
narratives.

War Stories

Like most of her contemporaries, Lowell was strongly affected by
the war of 1914–18, and she wrote a number of poems in response to
it. The section "War Pictures" in *Men, Women and Ghosts,* deals directly with the current struggle in Europe, while "Bronze Tablets"
goes back to the Napoleonic era, and of course war figures impor-
tantly in the background of such poems as "Patterns" and "Pickthorn
Manor." In *Can Grande's Castle,* Lowell examines various international
conflicts; *Pictures of the Floating World* contains a group of meditative
lyrics called "As Toward War"; and her uncollected *Phantasms of War*
poems are largely anti-German propaganda, which she thought of as
her contribution to the war effort.[12] In "Lead Soldiers" and "A Ballad
of Footmen," on the other hand, from the "War Pictures" poems in
Men, Women and Ghosts, she attacks the needless bloodshed and waste
of war and the human savagery that makes war possible. Poetry, art
in general, she believed, could not stand aloof from the truths of war.

Lowell's war stories, however, ranging from propagandistic verse
to epic, are very uneven, with many of them falling far short of her
best work. The pacifist stance of "A Ballad of Footmen" suffers from
inappropriate, doggerellike lines. "Bombardment," a "War Picture"
in polyphonic prose and a poem Lowell defended vigorously, is a

melodramatic failure, though apparently it made for good theatrics when Lowell read it aloud. In "Malmaison," however, Lowell provides a subtle, sensitive portrait of the Empress Josephine during the Napoleonic wars. As Josephine changes from Napoleon's beloved to one of the psychological casualties of his wars, she is as passionate and seductive as the roses that bloom in the gardens of Malmaison, and as transient and fragile as their fading petals. In her glory she even replaces the roses as a symbol of passion: "The roses have faded at Malmaison, nipped by the frost. What need for roses? Smooth, open petals—her arms. Fragrant, outcurved petals—her breasts. He rises like a sun above her, stooping to touch the petals, press them wider. Eagles. Bees. What are they to open roses!" (*C*, 114). When Napoleon turns from her, and Josephine suffers like a rose deprived of the sun, Lowell renders her emotional torment through a technique that verges on stream of consciousness:

Over the glass domes of the hot-houses drenches the rain. Behind her a clock ticks—ticks again. The sound knocks upon her thought with the echoing shudder of hollow vases. She places her hands on her ears, but the minutes pass, knocking. Tears in Malmaison. And years to come each knocking by, minute after minute. Years, many years, and tears, and cold pouring rain.
"I feel as though I had died, and the only sensation I have is that I am no more."
Rain! Heavy, thudding rain!

(*C*, 115)

The roselike woman has become an empty vase, who nonetheless consoles herself with "two hundred and twenty dresses" and who plagues her ex-husband with her unpaid bills (*C*, 115). Her rich garden and her loneliness recall those of the woman in "Patterns," but Josephine is a more complex and perhaps a more fully realized character because her frustrations make her avaricious and materialistic as well as tragic.

One of Lowell's best war stories, "Written on the Reverse," appeared in her last book, *Ballads for Sale*. A monologue in vigorous, colloquial blank verse, it is about the passion and death of a lieutenant in World War I, as remembered by his captain and friend. The lieutenant, a married man, has become involved with another woman—a "tawdry intrigue," according to the speaker, who sees the lieutenant as an honest, clumsy, middle-aged dreamer taken in by a worldly opportunist. Convinced that before long the lieutenant's "charmer would draw him farther in / To cheques of somewhat high denomination" (*C*, 566), the captain is irritated by his folly: "What right had he to be so innocent / To whip a tawdry intrigue up to poetry / And set me shivering who had not got it" (*C*, 565). And of course the captain is jealous of his friend, who is innocent enough to believe that he and his lover are like Nelson and Lady Hamilton, or even Anthony and Cleopatra. Recognizing, however, that his love has become an "epic" for the lieutenant, the captain grows to admire him as someone "greatly larger / Than I could have believed" (*C*, 566), even though he cannot wholly approve of the affair.

In ways not fully comprehensible to the speaker, the lieutenant becomes the ideal self he had created in his imagination, an innocent who remains faithful to his epic love, even though he is almost certainly unfaithful to his wife. He responds to war in the same terms—idealizing it, believing in the possibilities of heroism. He was "such a baby," in the captain's eyes, "Playing the soldier in a uniform," but "playing it damned well. . . . We had no better in the regiment" (*C*, 565). Even when he meets the grim reality of war, and is killed by a bit of shell piercing one of his lungs, it is on his own heroic terms: "He met that shell toting a wounded sergeant / Through our barrage" (*C*, 566). The lieutenant dies, with the war raging round him, "Coughing, and spitting, and whimpering" his lover's name, in what Lowell very skillfully avoids turning into a melodramatic or predictable scene. The speaker is almost tight-lipped. His admiration for the lieutenant is tempered by his knowledge that lover and wife have survived very well without him, and he is unable to reconcile his impressions of the man as a self-made hero and a self-deluded dupe:

> Tough luck? Oh, I don't know. He had his time.
> When the delirium struck him, I covered my ears,
> Hearing a man like that is too close cornered,
> Like something naked hurting you with beauty.
> It ended then for him, but I came home.
> His wife was cool and stately as a widow.
> The talcum-powder lady changed her man.
> And yet I think the person was an artist
> To carve a hero out of what he was
> When she first ran across him. I wonder sometimes
> What she can think about it. As for me,
> I always give it up at just this point.
> Poor dear old chap, God bless his silly soul.
>   (*C*, 566)

And thus the poem ends on a complex emotional chord of bafflement, love for the lieutenant, the old irritation, and a new understanding of the lieutenant's lover. Ultimately, the lieutenant emerges as someone who broke out of the expected patterns to create his own rules, and though the pattern called war does kill him, he "had his time." For the real loss is the speaker's, who will "never get the joy that fellow had" (*C,* 566), and whose character and emotions Lowell deftly evokes from this tale about another man. "Written on the Reverse" is a modern poem of considerable achievement, artistically equal to the well-known "Patterns," and it deserves to be much more widely read and debated than it is.

Chapter Five

Narrative Poetry II: Histories and Myths

Most of the narratives discussed so far express the personal emotions of individual men and women. The narratives in *Can Grande's Castle* and *Legends* deal more with impersonal forces—symbols rather than individualized characters, historical movements rather than personal feeling. Having already begun to explore the possibilities of history in such poems as the "Bronze Tablets" chronicles of *Men, Women and Ghosts,* Lowell wanted to expand her material and enlarge her scope. In *Can Grande's Castle,* her attempt to write an epic of civilization, she used the past to clarify the present, which she felt was too close to personal experience to be understood without the aid of history. Though not, Lowell said, a book about war in "the strict sense of the word," it is an imaginative response to World War I as the most recent instance of man's epic struggle to preserve his civilization. Finding herself in "the midst of war," Lowell turned "to the experiences of other men in other wars," and she discovered that "war itself is an expression of life, a barbaric expression on one side calling for an heroic expression on the other."[1] Her epic, as she conceives of it, is of civilization's chances for survival.

In the preface to *Legends,* Lowell defines civilization as man's "slowly acquired knowledge of how he can best exist in company with his fellows on the planet called Earth." As man gains "a measure of understanding," he attempts to express it through tales, creating legends: "they are bits of fact, or guesses at fact, pressed into the form of a story and flung out into the world as markers of how much ground has been travelled."[2] *Legends* is Lowell's most sustained use of myth and folktale to describe what today we call archetypal patterns of human experience, and it is, in effect, another excursion into the past—and into the truth-carrying power of the symbols of human imagination. She also wanted to prove, in both books, although it should not have been necessary, that she did not have to rely on autobiographical experiences for her poetry.

Can Grande's Castle:
Lowell's Experiment in Epic

Can Grande's Castle is at once a frustrating and a dazzling book. Composed of four poems in polyphonic prose, its historical scale is immense. "Sea-Blue and Blood-Red" deals with the love affair of Lord Nelson and Lady Hamilton during the turbulent Napoleonic era. "Guns as Keys: and the Great Gate Swings" describes Perry's journey to Japan and the opening of that nation to American trade. "Hedge Island" celebrates the days of the old mail coaches in England, just before the coming of the railroad and industrialization. "The Bronze Horses," the longest of the poems and virtually a book in itself, traces the history of four sculptured horses from ancient Rome, to medieval Constantinople, to Venice at the end of the eighteenth century, and finally to Venice again during World War I. Each of the poems shows Lowell's virtuoso ability for accurate description, with which she turns historical eras into a series of vivid scenes, as in this episode of the horse race from the Constantinople section of "The Bronze Horses":

They have reached the Grand Stand again, and the chariots are shut and barred in their stalls. The multitude, rustling as though they were paper being folded, settles down into their seats. The President drops a napkin, the bars are unlocked, and the chariots in a double rush take the straight at top speed, Blue leading, Green saving up for the turn at the curve. Round the three cones at the end, Blue on one wheel, Green undercutting him. Blue turns wide to right himself, takes the outside course and flashes up the long edge so that you cannot count two till he curves again. Down to the Green Corner, Blue's off horses slipping just before the cones, one hits the pole, loses balance and falls, drags a moment, catches his feet as the chariot slows for the circle, gathers, plunges, and lunges up and on, while the Greens on the benches groan and curse.

(*C*, 183)

Writing like that—energetic, detailed, fast-paced—dazzled Lowell's early readers, and its impact can be felt today.

But the spectacular energy of the polyphonic prose raised, as it still does, a difficulty, in that it tends to overwhelm with the sheer force of spectacle. One early critic complained that the "style of this polyphonic prose hits one in the face all the time. It is very emphatic, staccato, abrupt, so that one feels as if he had been shouted at

through a hundred pages."[3] And Conrad Aiken, who conceded that
Can Grande's Castle was "an astonishing book," also objected to the
unrelieved intensity of the imagery, especially of color: "So persistent
is Miss Lowell's colouristic attitude, so nearly unvaried is her habit of
presenting people, things, and events in terms of colour alone, that
presently she has reduced one to a state of colour blindness. Image
kills image, hue obliterates hue, one page erases another. And when
this point has been reached one realizes that Miss Lowell's polyphonic
prose has little else to offer. Its sole *raison d'être* is its vividness."[4]
Lowell was frequently charged with being concerned only with exter-
nals, even in those poems in which she did not consciously use the
unrelated or externalist method. But though *Can Grande's Castle* is
replete with surface image, the effect is not always what Aiken
claims. While the racehorses are thrashing in the streets, the bronze
horses stand over them on top of the Hippodrome, poised and serene
in the perfection of an art that transcends the struggles of time. And
while Constantinople divides into rival factions contending over the
race, a far more serious contest is looming, as the Venetians and the
French prepare their invasion of the city. Similarly, in another vividly
described scene, a balloon rises above Venice during carnival time; it
"floats without direction; suspended in movement, it hangs"—until
it finally rises and dwindles to a speck (*C, 192*). In the meantime,
Napoleon is marching across Italy toward the celebrating Venetians
who, Lowell says, see only a beautiful toy and not the awful vision it
gives them of the future. Little more than a century later, other
specks "seem to hang" and "hover without direction" over Venice (*C,
199*). In a fine use of lateral imagery, the balloons have become Italian fighter planes attempting to intercept Austrian bombers. Rather
than killing each other, such images take on metaphoric and com-
pound significance.[5]

Nevertheless, Aiken is right about Lowell's use of color to render
character, especially in "Sea-Blue and Blood-Red," the poem in
which characterization is most important, and in which Lowell does
little to individualize Nelson and Lady Hamilton. Instead, she describes them largely through their associations with specific colors,
and introduces a metaphoric loom to emphasize that their lives are
being woven for them with red and blue threads: "Sea-blue, the
warp; but the thread of the woof is bolted red. . . . The shuttle
shoots, the shuttle weaves. The red thread to the blue thread cleaves.
The web is plaiting which nothing unreaves" (*C, 156–57*). Through-

out the poem, blue is associated with the sea and the sky, which surround Nelson's career as a naval commander. It represents duty, Nelson's public life and role. His uniform at Trafalgar is a blue coat; and it is "Blue water" that calls him away from Lady Hamilton for Trafalgar—at which point the blue shuttle tears through the red (*C,* 160). In battle, blue gives way to red, and as Nelson's duty necessitates the spilling of blood, so is his perception divided by blue and red: "Signal flags are of all colours, but the Admiral sees only the red. It beats above him, outlined against the salvia-blue sky. A crimson blossom sprung from his heart, the banner royal of his Destiny struck out sharply against the blue of Heaven" (*C,* 161). Just before the battle and all its unknown chances, Nelson's world changes momentarily to blue again, as he determines to do his duty despite his foreboding of death; "What is it that haunts his mind? He is blinded by red, blood-red fading to rose, smeared purple, blotted out by blue" (*C,* 161). But when he takes his fatal wound, the world becomes "all red now":

Red blood in a flood before his eyes. Red from horizon to zenith, crushing down like beaten metal. The Admiral falls to his knees, to his side, and lies there, and the crimson glare closes over him, a cupped inexorable end. "They have done for me at last, Hardy. My back-bone is shot through."

The blue thread is snapped and the bolt falls from the loom. Weave, shuttle of the red thread. Weave over and under yourself in a scarlet ecstasy. It is all red now he comes to die. (*C,* 161)

Red is also the color of passion and sexual desire, and it is the symbol of Lady Hamilton. Her "heart beats blood, not water"; her "blood is alive. The red of it stains a bright band across the pages of history" (*C,* 156). Though she wears a blue ribbon in honor of Nelson's victory at Aboukir Bay, she appears to Nelson as "a mist of rose and silver" (*C,* 157). As Nelson's passion for her grows, a redness spreads across Naples from the windows of her rooms: "All Naples is red to the Admiral, but the core of crimson is the Palazzo Sesso, in whose windows, at night, the silver stars flash so brightly. 'Crimson and silver,' thinks the Admiral, 'O Emma, Emma Hamilton!' " (*C,* 157).

If blue colors the surface world of sea and sky, the source of red is hidden, like blood, and underground within the lava of Vesuvius, which glowers over Naples like a red eye. Lady Hamilton is drawn to the forbidding force of the volcano, identifying with it to become a queen of night and fire: "A tossing fountain of blood-red jets, it sets

her hair flicking into the air like licking flamelets of a burning au-
reole. Blood-red is everywhere. She wears it as a halo and diadem"
(C, 154). In effect, she has merged and become one with the fiery
energy of the mountain, almost a demonic figure whom Nelson, in
his infatuation, persists in seeing as a saint—"Santa Emma," he calls
her (C, 158). In a suggestive and precise use of symbols, "Blood-red
is everywhere" in the Vesuvius scene near the beginning of the poem,
and it is "all red now" at the end after Trafalgar. The destructive
forces let loose by war are thus linked to the elemental furnace within
the earth, and red combines passion and death. Nelson, speaking of
Lady Hamilton, "sees Vesuvius" just before he dies (C, 162); and
Lowell describes Lady Hamilton's passions in terms that are equally
suited to the volcano or a naval battle: "She is aflame, scorching with
red and gold fires, a torch of scarlet and ochre, a meteor of sulphur
and chrome dashed with vermilion" (C, 158). Nelson, destined to die
in the red world of war while performing his duty, is irresistibly
drawn to Lady Hamilton's scorching and illicit passion—his surrender to her appropriately described as an overcoming of blue by red:

> Over the satin-wood table, the Admiral and the Ambassadress sit in con-
> sultation, and red fire flares between them across its polished surface. "My
> adorable, unfortunate Queen! Dear, dear Queen!" Lady Hamilton's eyes are
> carbuncles burning into the Admiral's soul. He is dazzled, confused, used
> to the glare on blue water he thinks he sees it now. It is Duty and Kings.
> Caste versus riff-raff. The roast beef of old England against fried frogs' legs.
>   Red, blood-red, figures the weaving pattern, red blushing over blue,
> flushing the fabric purple, like lees of wine. (C, 157–58)

It is wrong, surely, to say that Lowell gives us colors instead of characters, for both Nelson and Lady Hamilton are powerfully drawn.
Rather, she uses colors to portray the clash between duty and desire,
and to show that, while her lovers were heroic figures who flamed
across their time, they were also puppetlike, at the mercy of forces
larger than themselves, which controlled what they did and desired.
    The clash in "Guns as Keys: and the Great Gate Swings" is be-
tween racial attitudes. Perry's journey to Japan forces a confrontation
between the commercialistic, practical West and the aesthetic, phil-
osophical East. In the first of the poem's two parts, moreover, Lowell
contrasts and balances the two cultures by alternating polyphonic
prose for the West with free verse for scenes in Japan. Distant events
are thus made to occur simultaneously without lessening the cultural

distance between Americans and Japanese. In the first juxtaposition, Perry is just leaving America.

> My! How she throws the water off from her bows, and how those paddle-wheels churn her along at the rate of seven good knots! You are a proud lady, Mrs. *Mississippi*, curtseying down Chesapeake Bay, all a-flutter with red white and blue ribbons.

> At Mishima in the Province of Kai,
> Three men are trying to measure a pine tree
> By the length of their outstretched arms.
> Trying to span the bole of a huge pine tree
> By the spread of their lifted arms.
> Attempting to compress its girth
> Within the limit of their extended arms.
>   (C, 162–63)

Besides the difference in form, the language shifts from the colloquial American speech of the polyphonic prose to the subdued almost stately diction of the free verse.

Language and action are an index to the national characters. While the Americans, with daring enterprise, are circling the globe, the Japanese are attempting what seems a far more limited action: to join hands around a tree. The busyness and progress of the one contrast with the slow motion and concentrated stasis of the other. In fact, the free verse lines themselves make a full circle, ending where they began, with the three men trying to form a circle. While Perry is in the process of moving history forward and changing the future of Japan, the Japanese fail in their attempt at an enclosure. But the Japanese also show a harmony with nature lacking in the Americans. Perry's ship has to battle with the sea—nosing her way through it, panting, thrusting forward—to cross it as quickly as possible. The Japanese see enough to occupy themselves in the width of a single tree—imitating, or being imitated by, clouds that wreathe the top of Fuji. Again, image does not kill image. The action over Fuji parallels and expands the efforts of the men—there are gaps in the clouds; the men's hands break apart. The reader, perhaps, gets a double warning that Japan cannot be easily compassed.

The juxtapositions—in another instance, Perry is writing to his wife and a Japanese merchant spends the night with a courtesan—create tension and suspense over the confrontation of the two cultures as the Americans approach Japan. As Perry is about to make the last leg of his journey, part 1 ends with a finely narrated ritual execution of a Japanese warrior by his former pupil. Part 2 is in polyphonic prose only. Perry is in Japan, which will become Westernized, and Lowell was undoubtedly correct to describe it now with the polyphonic prose she used for the West, although the second part is not nearly as good as the first with its contrasting voices. Nor are the Japanese characterized by the dignified postures and aesthetic charm of part 1, but become mostly animallike and inept. Lowell did have a deep appreciation of Japanese culture, however, and she knew that when the great gates capitulated to Perry, they let out as much as they let in—a historical truth which she explicitly makes the theme of her poem:

A locomotive in pay for a Whistler; telegraph wires buying a revolution; weights and measures and Audubon's birds in exchange for fear. Yellow monkey-men leaping out of Pandora's box, shaking the rocks of the Western coastline. Golden California bartering panic for prints. The dressing-gowns of a continent won at the cost of security. Artists and philosophers lost in the hour-glass sand pouring through an open Gate.

(C, 172)

And though it is impossible to state which culture has exerted the greater influence over the other in the transmission of ideas after Perry, Lowell seems to give the Japanese artistic spirit the last word over confident American commercialism in two final scenes. A young Japanese commits suicide after carving on the trunk of a tree his belief that the universe is "unknowable" (C, 172). The episode recalls the attempt of the three men to measure a tree, and suggests that, despite industrialization, something essential remains in the Japanese character. The second scene is an exhibition of Whistler's paintings, showing the influence, if not the conquest, of Japanese art over the Western imagination.[6]

The triumph of art, its value as the highest and most enduring achievement of civilization, is the subject of "The Bronze Horses," probably the most ambitious poem that Lowell ever wrote. Its four parts cover nearly two thousand years of Western history, from Rome in the first century A.D., to Venice in 1915. The sculptured horses, older than ancient Rome, are Lowell's clearest symbol in *Can Grande's Castle* of what she referred to in her preface as the "heroic expression" of life answering or countering the "barbaric" expressions of war, ri-

valry, and greed. The horses transcend time and stand above the
petty values and changing fortunes of man. Literally, they are always
situated high in the air, where they seem to hover between earth and
eternity, the baser and the more divine natures of man, as when we
first see them in Rome:

> One foot paws in the air. A step, and they will lance into the air, Pega-
> sus-like, stepping the wind. But they do not take the step. They wait—
> poised, treading Rome as they trod Alexandria, as they trod the narrow is-
> land of Cos. The spokes of the *quadriga* wheels flash, but they do not turn.
> They burn like day-stars above the Arch of Nero. The horses poise over
> Rome, a constellation of morning, triumphant above Emperors, proud, in-
> different, enduring, relentlessly spurning the hot dust of Rome. Hot dust
> clouds up about them, but not one particle sticks to their gilded manes.
> Dust is nothing, a mere smoke of disappearing hours. Slowly they trot for-
> ward without moving, and time passes and passes them, brushing along
> their sides like wind.
>
> (*C*, 177–78)

In fact, time does change the horses; they are scratched and they lose
their *quadriga* or chariot in the sack of Constantinople. But compared
to the cities they watch over—whose wealth is plundered, whose artifacts turn to dust—they are timeless and survive the fall of empires.

They survive as if they were elemental, like earth, air, water, and
fire. Each of the four parts of "The Bronze Horses" contains a preface
on the elements as destructive and creative powers which give rise to
and erase what Lowell calls "the seasons of man" (*C*, 187)—the
phases of history. Man uses the elements to destroy and is destroyed
by them. The ground shakes with the marching feet of Rome's returning armies, who have crossed earth and sea to plunder other nations. The Venetians attack Constantinople by water and set it on
fire. Venice burns after Austria has attacked it by air. But fire, which
destroys, also makes possible the art of the bronze horses: "Fire
melts, and the absence of Fire cools and freezes. So are metals fused
in twisted flames and take on a form other than that they have
known, and this new form shall be to them rebirth and making."
Civilization and most of its artifacts, in effect, are known "only between burning and burning" (*C*, 177). The horses, however, are able
to "mock at fire" (*C*, 181). As works of art they become their own
fire. And as changes in the elements—the "ancient dance," forward
and back, of earth, water and sky (*C*, 181)—mark the passing of

time, the fusion, the rebirth, of the elements in the bronze horses holds time still.

Reappearing at crucial moments throughout the poem, the horses serve as the "return" or recurring motif that Lowell felt was necessary to poetry, and they provide a vantage point from which to view the activity below them. But essentially unchanging themselves, eternally frozen like a figure on Keats's Grecian urn, they have only limited narrative possibilities outside of their symbolic import. The chief interest of the poem, at least the bulk of its telling, is concerned with the teeming life on the streets and waterways of the different cities. Lowell uses shifting points of view to describe this, creating a newsreel effect of multiple scenes and voices, and anticipating the more elaborate work of Dos Passos and the modern splicing techniques now used by the media. Panorama—the ascent of the balloon, the final departure of the horses back to Rome—alternates with close-up. Often, Lowell situates herself in the middle of a crowded thoroughfare to give a Whitmanesque catalog of people, artifacts, and trades:

A gentleman in a buttercup-coloured coat goes by with a bouquet. A sea-green gown brocaded with cherry and violet stays an instant before a stall to buy a packet of ambergris. Pilgrims with staffs and cockles knock the stones as they shuffle along, a water-carrier shouts out a song. A scarlet sacristan jingles his keys; purple robes of justices saunter at ease. Messer Goldoni hustles by to a rehearsal, and three famous *castrati,* i Signori Pacchierotti, Aprili, Rubenelli, rustle their mantles and adjust their masks, ogling the ladies with gold lorgnons. Blind men sniffle into flageolets, marionette men hurry on to a distant Campo in a flurry of cotton streamers. If Venice is a flowing of water, it is also a flowing of people. All Europe runs into this wide square. (*C,* 190)

Not only is the scene visualized; it is heard in such verbs as "knock," "jingles," "rustle," and "sniffle." Sometimes, striving for greater immediacy, Lowell blends her authorial voice into dialogues between Romans, Byzantines, or Venetians.

In effect, Lowell opened all the stops of her polyphonic prose to support her belief that it could become the form of the modern epic. She proved it capable of complexity and nuance, and she achieved some startling tonal and cinematic effects. But *Can Grande's Castle* does not succeed as an epic, and there is considerable justification, especially in the overlong "Bronze Horses," for the sense of fatigue expressed by such critics as Tupper and Aiken. The polyphonic form itself need not result in the excessive details and minor incidents that mar "The Bronze Horses," but it probably encouraged their use. For a poem so concerned with history, moreover, "The Bronze Horses" shows little sense of history as a shaping force, of the influence upon people of different times, and it contains much redundancy, as the follies of the Romans reappear virtually unchanged in the later eras, and as Romans, Byzantines, and Venetians all speak and react in very much the same way. An epic theme—whether it be the opposition of life's heroic and barbaric expressions or something else—does not sufficiently emerge, while the symbolic value of the artistic horses, once established, does not suggestively resonate. And though individual scenes have strong dramatic or lyrical impact, the poem as a whole does not. Lowell was much more successful with the juxtapositions in "Guns as Keys," and with the lurid and sensual lights and shadows of "Sea-Blue and Blood-Red."

But Lowell's principal difficulties come from the form itself, and appear in the prosody that she gave it because of her determination to get polyphonic prose accepted as a form of poetry. She claimed that when the poems in *Can Grande's Castle* were read aloud, such poetic devices as rhyme added to the tonal effect of the whole without calling attention to themselves.[7] But, as was true of her earlier attempts with the form, the rhymes in fact often stand out obtrusively. A section from the passage quoted above is typical of many. "Pilgrims with staffs and cockles knock the stones as they shuffle along, a water-carrier shouts out a song. A scarlet sacristan jingles his keys; purple robes of justices saunter at ease." The purpose of "along" and "at ease," besides their slight tonal contribution, is primarily to complete rhymes; and while pilgrims might possibly have or carry cockles (mollusk shells? cocklebur?), it is almost certain that they do so here only for the sound effect of "cockles" and "knock." Lowell, of course, may well have chosen sound over sense in what she thought of as an orchestral form. Her technique falters because the sound effects themselves often lack originality and creative skill. Her rhymes do not blend into the prose, and Aiken rightly criticized the following alliterative display as amateurish: "Such a pounding, pummelling, pitching, pointing, piercing, pushing, pelting, poking, panting, punching, parrying, pulling, prodding, puking, piling, passing, you never did see."[8] Rather than showing the elastic freedom that Lowell identified with polyphonic prose, this and other overelaborations of technique for its own sake seem arbitrary and artificial. Self-conscious rhymes and alliterations do not make polyphonic prose a form of poetry; and as Aiken notes, they often keep it below the level of good prose.[9] Conversely, the best passages use such devices sparingly, or dispense with them altogether.

Lowell herself must have grown tired or dissatisfied with the form, for after *Can Grande's Castle* she wrote little in polyphonic prose. But if she was unable to make it the form of the modern epic, she did use it to explore nontraditional methods of storytelling in a significant, if unsuccessful, attempt at epic. By basing narrative on fragments and dislocated episodes, instead of continuous plot, and rendering character through metaphor, image, and tableau, or turning character itself into crowd, *Can Grande's Castle* gives an early instance of a number of innovations that have since become common in literature and film.

Legends and the Uses of Myth

Legends is no less innovative in its way, and it shows a more instinctive grasp of symbol and underlying meanings, or what Lowell called the "substratum of reality"—the imagination's understanding of the truths of life before these have been expounded by science.[10] Acknowledging that she had adapted and not originated the stories, she found the material for most of them in ethnological and literary studies, from which she also took a strong impression of the similarity of certain legends "among a wide variety of peoples."[11] She was, of course, neither a folklorist nor a comparative mythologist, and not all eleven poems in *Legends* work successfully with myth or archetypal matter. Those that do, however, are among the best of Lowell's narratives.

"Memorandum Confided by a Yucca to a Passion-Vine" is a myth about the origins of the spots on the moon, and derives from a Peruvian legend that the marks were left by the paws of a fox who fell in love with the moon and touched it. Lowell, too, loved the moon, made it the subject or inspiration of a number of her poems, and was drawn to Keats as a fellow moon-worshipper. The fox, one of her more memorable and rascally characters, makes an arduous quest to reach the moon's home in Cuzco, where he persuades a Virgin of the Sun to lead him to the moon's temple. There, after the moon has disrobed and stands naked and shining before a group of dead Inca mothers, the fox bursts from the Virgin's grasp and assaults it. A burst of thunder and lightning repels the fox, but its prints remain on the moon.

There is no mistaking the sexual, animal nature of the fox's assault. Lowell calls him a "Satyr fox"; his prints are "obscene" (*C*, 251); he attempts to rape the moon. She first appears to him, before his quest, as a beautiful, naked woman; and as her body sways above him, his eyes greedily devour "the curving undulations. . . . With hot tongue he pants upon the splendour / Of this marble beauty, imperious and unashamed" (*C*, 246). Given the sensuality projected by the moon, who "shimmers" and exposes her breasts and thighs, perhaps it is no wonder that the fox is sexually aroused—the human speaker in "Fool O' the Moon," enflamed by a similar sight, says that he has "lain with Mistress Moon" (*C*, 466). Numerous sexual images also characterize the moon's city of Cuzco. It is the home of the passion-vine—"Scarlet-flashing" in the sun (*C*, 247). And as dead Inca women perform the rites of the moon, dead Inca men invoke the sun in what Lowell calls a "phallic chorus":

> Warm our meadows,
> Bless the seed-ears.
> Man and woman,
> Beast and lizard,
> Feathered people,
> Whales and fishes,
> All implore thee,
> Clement God-head,
> To make fruitful
> These thy creatures.
> String their sinews
> Ripe for power,
> Quicken wombs and
> Eggs and rootlets.
> Be the Father,
> The Begetter.
>   (*C*, 248)

The fertility song of the "dead" men—men lacking the fructifying power of the sun—is followed by the petition to the moon of a barren woman, the Virgin of the Sun. The song has aroused her sexuality, and fearing that she will violate her vows, she asks the moon for strength and calmness. Otherwise, let her be annihilated in a moment of ecstatic surrender:

> Give me thunder,
> Give me lightning,
> Break me on a green-stone anvil,
> So the flower of my body
> Blow to loveliness a moment.
> I am past my holding, Mama Quilla,
> In the night I smell the strong-scented blossoms of the daturas,
> And my heart snares me in its loneliness.
>
> (C, 249)

Her prayer, and especially the reference to thunder and lightning, foreshadows the final effort and destruction of the fox.

The fox understands the frustrated longings of the Virgin. The sexuality she struggles against, he accepts as a part of his destiny, giving him a single-mindedness that makes him intensely alive as opposed to the dead Inca worshippers of the sun and moon—just as he is literally alive while the plants and insects in the Inca's garden are made of metal. The Inca men pray to the sun to impregnate nature; the fox attempts to copulate with the moon, appropriating to himself the masculine principle which the Incas worship in the sun, and seeking to unite with the feminine—the "Womb of peoples" (C, 251). He would incarnate in himself, make present in animal nature, powers that are in fact animal in nature, but which the Incas spiritualize and remove from man. The Virgin of the Sun accuses him of sacrilege, but the moon does not have the sacramental value for the fox that it does for her. The fox desires the moon strongly, "more than the monkeys of the Eastern forests / Desire dates," and he prizes her "more greatly than do the Aquarimas the shrunken skulls of their enemies" (C, 249). But as the images suggest, he does not idealize the moon. His object of worship is as sensual and finite as dates or skulls or foxes, and at the end, in a sign that the two are linked, the moon wears the mark of the fox. Lowell may call the fox "ghoulish" and portray him as a sly, lustful male seeking to defile the female, but her sympathy for the fox is also apparent. As a rebel, an advocate of authentic passion, the fox provides a necessary counterpoint to the abject Inca worshippers and to the sanctimonious, noli-me-tangere nudity of the moon. His perseverance makes a strong appeal for a demystified physical sexuality; and like other passionate characters in Lowell's poems, his restless energy opposes the sexual patterns that control others.

"The Statue in the Garden" offers another version of sexual entrapment and conflict. A young writer, Julius, tired of human companionship, has purchased a secluded house and garden where he can live alone. One day he buys a lead statue of a pretty maiden for his garden, and pretending that they are lovers he slips his diamond ring on her finger. The ring will not come off when he tries to remove it. Later, after he has been away for a month and met a human woman, Hildegarde, the statue comes to his room to declare her love for him and claim him as her betrothed. Julius, of course, is disbelieving and stunned, but it is no dream. The statue visits him often, pressing against his door and beating her hands upon it, tempting Julius to leave his known, human world for her different, unknown existence. Finally Julius decides to find her a mate and buys another statue, a man with a scythe. The male statue becomes jealous of the lead woman's love for Julius, and after a furious chase involving all three, Julius escapes, decides to sell his house, and will return to normal society.

The tale has a long history and has been frequently retold. Lowell's source was Burton's *Anatomy of Melancholy,* where the lead woman is a statue of Venus who, on the man's wedding night, puts herself between him and his human wife.[12] Lowell's version omits that scene and does not make the statue a goddess, but it is much longer and more detailed than Burton's, which takes less than a page. Her object, she said, "was to show the lure of the aesthetic, and how inhuman it might make a person, who could only be saved by the return to human love and human desires."[13] The tale is a warning against solitary indulgence in beauty and personal tastes at the expense of social intercourse:

> [Julius] was tired out with the old routine
> Of man and man, now something between
> Held him away and apart. Intense
> Became his ultra-commonsense,
> And he was happy and preened himself
> On being an unusual sort of elf,
> Not feeling the need of his fellows at all.
> Julius was riding for a fall.
>
> (C, 281)

He is too self-satisfied and has chosen, not a healthy independence, but an irresponsible escape from life.

But Lowell's narrative reveals more than her stated moral intentions. By deserting human society and choosing objects instead of people for his companions, Julius begins to cross the threshold to an eerily surrealistic world. A large old cabinet stands in the shop where Julius finds the statues. Their later strange behavior is anticipated by Julius's experience with the cabinet, which also seems to have a life of its own:

> Did Julius hear a rusty sound which quivered
> Down the old cabinet, cracking in the heat?
> Those grinning dwarfs pursued him to the street,
> He felt their obscene jaws stretching and gobbling.
>
> (C, 283)

When Julius returns to buy the second statue, the dwarfs on the cabinet mock him even more, and the cabinet has become a grotesque reproduction of Julius's garden, which it turns into a garden filled with snakes:

> He saw the green snake-tree
> Convulsed, contorted, and swaying.
> He saw it was his sycamore
> As he had never seen it.
> The leaves were clapping and sighing.
> The leaves and the faces together,
> And the long snake boughs with heads
> Which swept in terrible circles.
>
> (C, 287)[14]

Later, when Julius is being chased by the statue that loves him and the statue with the scythe that would kill him, his garden reproduces the cabinet, his sycamore trees changing into "white and hovering snakes" (C, 289).

The expert use of surrealistic imagery adds greatly to the suspense and implications of "The Statue in the Garden." Julius is both tempted and horrified by that strange other world suggested by the cabinet and vividly present in the two statues. In one sense, they threaten him with insanity; to accept them as real is to lose touch with reality, and Julius realizes, well before the chase scene, that he will see snakes in his sycamores if he returns the lead woman's love.

In a more important sense, though, that other world is a different version of reality, foreign to reason or buried by time in the unconscious. It shows reality, even the familiar, as Julius has "never seen it," and it challenges him to enlarge his perceptions, to undertake a mental quest into the unknown without losing his grip on normalcy. "Julius, Julius," the narrator asks, "are you man or superman? / Can you pass the nether space / And keep a clue for returning?" (*C,* 289). One of the meanings of "clue" is the ball of thread which guides one out of a labyrinth, giving Julius's adventure the heroic connotations of a superman and increasing the sense of peril to him as a man. As the strange snake-filled garden and even stranger love offered Julius suggest, the quest takes him from the regulated Apollonian world he has physically left and into a Dionysian realm, which is evil because it is antagonistic to social order and attractive or tempting because it is forbidden. Still holding to his former values—he performs the mock marriage ceremony with the statue—while the statue woos him, Julius fluctuates; he sees the statue's love as having "at once the grace of flowers / And the horror of serpents" (*C,* 289). He is not sure if her wooing has brought him pleasure or pain, and his mixture of feelings includes a hurt that she stayed away from him for three days after he provided her with a male companion. But Julius is not superman and no Dionysian. The Apollonian world prevails, Julius returns to conventional life, and the two statues lie sunken in a lake.

Lowell provides some further, more specific hints about the nature of the lead woman. We see, for instance, that she is not a Hildegarde. Julius feels "no qualm" about returning to Hildegarde: "Some things are certain, Hildegarde is one" (*C,* 291). There will be no surprises or ambiguities with Hildegarde, and presumably, no fierce display of emotion such as Julius awoke in the statue. Julius bought the statue so that he could make love to a woman without committing himself, and be free to play the lover's role in a mock marriage without risking a response. He pretends the statue is flesh and blood and woos her in his "best poetic style"—it is, Lowell says, nothing but sex that is driving him:

> Now 'twas nothing but sex
> Deprived its due reason, which set Julius sighing
> Before a lead statue instead of complying
> With all mystic wisdom and seeking a woman
> Who, whatever she lacked, would be certainly human.
> (*C,* 284)

Julius does not desire a human woman, however, but rather the unchanging, pretty image of one that he can love on his own terms. The statue's ardent and surprising response—her passions are unleashed, not regulated, by the mock ceremony—exposes Julius to feelings that he did not expect from his "bride," and with which he does not know how to cope after he has aroused them. Thus, the unknown Dionysian other—the familiar as he has never seen it—is female sexuality as it is capable of expressing itself, and as such it both tempts and threatens Julius; and perhaps it is his own unacknowledged sexuality pursuing him in the form of the sexually aroused and jealous scythe-wielder. The poem is rich in such suggestions and in irony too, as Julius retreats from what he thought would be the safe world of his fancies to the much less explosive and more predictable world of the human Hildegarde.

Lowell's favorite poem in *Legends* was "Many Swans," for which Damon says she read sixty-three volumes on Indian poetry and folklore. She found the main outline of the story in Franz Boas's transcription of a Kathlamet Indian sun myth.[15] In the Kathlamet text, a man sets out to visit the sun. After ten months, when he is near the place where the sun rises, he comes upon a hut filled with various weapons and artifacts—arrows, shields, animal skins, blankets, and beads. A girl explains that all these belong to her father's mother, an old woman who leaves the house all day and returns at night carrying a great shining thing—a sun symbol. The man lives for a long while as the husband of the girl, but eventually becomes homesick. The old woman offers him anything he wants from the skins, blankets, and ornaments in the hut, but he insists on the great shining thing, and when it is given him he leaves for his home with the thing hanging from him. At the first town, however, his uncle's town, the thing shakes in his hand and says, "We shall strike your town." The man goes mad and breaks the town and kills all its people. Then he realizes that the thing he wanted was bad and tries to throw it away, but it sticks to his flesh. He comes upon the town of another one of his uncles, and destroys it. Still he cannot take the thing off, nor can he break it. He destroys two more towns belonging to his uncles, and finally reaches his own town, where he kills all his family. Then the old woman appears to him, and saying that she tried to love him and wanted to be kind to his people, she removes the thing from him and leaves.

Lowell kept the basic tale, but introduced a number of significant changes and additions. Many Swans—her name for the man—reaches the country of the sun after he has shot all his arrows at the moon. The arrows form a ladder which he climbs for four days until he comes upon the young woman, who is now made a vegetation figure and named "Grass-Bush-and-Blossom."[16] His interest in her is primarily and explicitly sexual: he "hungered for the woman and could not wait" (*C*, 262). When she offers him the various possessions of the hut, he says that he wants her. And when the old woman, "The-One-Who-Walks-All-Over-the-Sky," finds the two of them lying together, she rebukes Many Swans: "You have not waited. . . . It is an evil beginning" (*C*, 263). He has shown no restraint and cannot control his appetites, which makes more plausible his later misuse of and corruption by the power of the sun symbol which he brings back to earth. In Lowell's version, Many Swans destroys three villages at widely spaced intervals, rather than a number of villages in rapid succession. The first village is his own. As he approaches it, congratulating himself on his cleverness and power, he changes into a pillar of smoke that bursts into fire and kills all his people, including his wife and children. He then goes into the wilderness, trying to free himself of the destructive thing and avoiding human contact, so that he will not kill again. He travels from the Pacific Northwest to the Great Plains, where, coming upon a village, he is unable to resist his need to speak with men, and the sun disk breaks into fire again. At last he is in the Southwest, where he witnesses the snake rituals of the Hopi. Though Many Swans feels strong enough now to control the thing, he is extremely cautious about entering the village, and in fact is turning away when he accidently meets a Hopi priest, and the thing sends out snakes of flame. Many Swans is now alone in the world, and after the old woman has taken the thing from him, he "looked at the desert. He looked at the dead town. He wept" (*C*, 273).

Lowell's ending is darker than that of the original, where, after the man has surveyed his ruined village, he builds a new house. Also, by enlarging her geography, she expands the tragedy from the destruction of a family to the destruction of the Indian race in the West. Lowell felt that the Indians especially suffered from the imposition of Christianity, which they did not understand and which deprived them of their own religions and customs, such as the finely described and intricate snake-dance.[17] Whatever her intentions were, however, the sun disk has no clear connection with Christianity, and no Europeans, symbolic or otherwise, appear in the poem. What Lowell does show is Indian culture being destroyed by something inherent within it. The Indians' close dependence on nature makes them vulnerable to such proverbially fickle forces as the sun and rain, which destroy as well as make life possible. In one scene, the madness that seizes Many Swans becomes the madness of war, intertribal destruction. Two groups of warriors ride toward each other, shooting arrows with terrible swiftness; and Many Swans hears them yelling,

> We who live are coming.
> Ai-ya-ya-yai!
> We are coming to kill.
> Ai-ya-ya-yai!
> We are coming with the snake arrows,
> We are coming with the tomahawks
> Which swallow their faces.
>
> (C, 267)

In effect, Many Swans is seeing himself multiplied, for the warriors' weapons "swallow" and turn into snakes like the flames in the sun disk on Many Swans. After the battle, there are no bodies, only arrows sticking out of the ground, and Many Swans avoids the spot because he believes the arrows "must be full of blood" (C, 267).

And of course, the destructive principle is in human nature—in Many Swan's love of power, his arrogance, his self-seeking choice of the shining thing instead of artifacts that would be more socially useful to his people. A fire-bringer, he is a Promethean figure, but in his selfishness and misjudgment he also resembles Midas; and rather than bringing a boon to his people, he creates a wasteland. He desired a power that was beyond his or any man's moral capacity; yet though he is erring and flawed, he is not irredeemably evil. In his remorse and penance—he fasts, he blackens his face and body—he undergoes spiritual growth. When he was descending from the sky country back to earth, he sang in self-praise of his own power and importance:

> I am going all round the world,
> I am at the center of the world,
> I am the post of the world,
> On account of what I am carrying in my hand.
>
> (C, 265)

When, instead of being the center of his world, he has become an outcast, he denounces his ambitions and learns to love other people and to see their importance. He swears, even upon the terrible thing he carries, to be a protector of the Hopi, for whom his love is so great that he cannot "stay still" (*C*, 270). Ultimately, he is an everyman, capable because of his human nature of turning his world into a hell, but also gaining, in his hard-won recognition of the dangers of power and the need for love, at least a partial redemption.

"Many Swans" is a powerful story. It is also Lowell's last important work in polyphonic prose, and almost certainly the best. From the opening lines, Lowell weaves tonal and rhythmic patterns into a language that is indeed polyphonic:

When the Goose Moon rose and walked upon a pale sky, and water made a noise once more beneath the ice on the river, his heart was sick with longing for the great good of the sun. One Winter again had passed, one Winter like the last. A long sea with waves biting each other under grey clouds, a shroud of snow from ocean to forest, snow mumbling stories of bones and driftwood beyond his red fire. He desired space, light; he cried to himself about himself, he made songs of sorrow and wept in the corner of his house. (*C*, 261)

"Is this poetry?" Padraic Colum asked.[18] Probably it is not, but perhaps it does not greatly matter. For it is beautiful prose, without the artificiality and self-consciousness that critics objected to in *Can Grande's Castle,* and it gives important information about Many Swans's character. For Colum, "Many Swans" suggests the way that stories might be told in Indian tepees. And Lawrence, who did not always find much to his liking in Lowell, said that the poem spoke from inside his own "unexplained soul."[19]

Chapter Six

Imagist and Impassionist: The Major Lyrics

While Lowell was writing the dramatic and narrative poems of *Men, Women and Ghosts, Can Grande's Castle,* and *Legends,* she was developing steadily as a lyric poet as well. We have seen how her discovery of imagism resulted in such finely wrought lyrics as "Taxi" and "Aubade" in *Sword Blades and Poppy Seed.* And although she often wrote with other ends in mind than those of imagism, the imagist principles taught her to focus on relevant detail and on sensory, nondiscursive language, and to value such qualities as concision and vividness as the identifying traits of modern poetry. *Pictures of the Floating World,* published in 1919, and *What's O'Clock,* published posthumously in 1925, show her often achieving these effects in her major lyrics—both in the shorter, suggestive picture poems most often associated with imagism, and in her longer lyrical meditations. By 1919, moreover, Lowell had begun to study seriously Japanese and Chinese poetry, a lifelong interest that would culminate in the collaborative translation with Florence Ayscough of Chinese lyrics in *Fir-Flower Tablets* (1921). The reticence, economy, and suggestiveness that Lowell found in such Oriental forms as the Japanese haiku reinforced the lessons of the imagists. Also, the emphasis, in imagist and much Oriental poetry, on objectivity, nuance, and exact language, taught Lowell to write of her own inmost feelings with greater detachment and to evoke, even from some of her most personal poems, strong transpersonal emotions.

Imagist Icons: "Written Pictures"

Although the imagists had denied that they were a school of painters, one of their aims was surely to make the reader "see"—to render particular moments and scenes out of colors and objects. And Lowell, who explored the analogies between poetry and music, was equally interested in what poetry could learn from painting—as her title, *Pic-*

tures of the Floating World, suggests. While writing *Fir-Flower Tablets,* moreover, she had to work with a form of verse that Florence Ays-cough translates as "Hanging-on-the-Wall Poems," or "Written Pictures," a form that specifically identifies poetry as a pictorial or visual art: "A beautiful thought perpetrated in beautiful handwriting and hung upon the wall to suggest a mental picture."[1] Lowell was not concerned with only the surface of things, but she was drawn to sensory and especially visual experience, and she wrote a number of descriptive poems that read essentially like word-paintings, such as "A Bather," from *Pictures of the Floating World:*

Thick dappled by circles of sunshine and fluttering shade,
Your bright, naked body advances, blown over by leaves,
Half-quenched in their various green, just a point of you showing,
A knee or a thigh, sudden glimpsed, then at once blotted into
The filmy and flickering forest, to start out again
Triumphant in smooth, supple roundness, edged sharp as white ivory,
Cool, perfect, with rose rarely tinting your lips and your breasts,
Swelling out from the green in the opulent curves of ripe fruit,
And hidden, like fruit, by the swift intermittence of leaves.

(C, 223)

Subtitled "After a Picture by Andreas Zorn," and delicately colored with green, ivory, and rose, "A Bather" is clearly more impression-istic than imagistic. It is also a composition, in the pictorial sense, using light and shade to reveal and obscure the body of the woman, which we see only in fragments or as ivorylike points in the flickering green. In the poem, of course, as opposed to the painting, the woman can move; and as she approaches the stream in which she will bathe, she weaves in and out of the forest, showing a sudden glimpse of knee or thigh, then blending back into the vegetation, only to start out again.

This image of the weaving human figure is carried beyond the purposes and the possibilities of mere surface description, however; it reveals the poem's theme, a vision of the woman's body as interwoven with nature—distinct like a bright thread in a dark cloth, but inseparable from the cloth. The woman's breasts are not merely like ripe fruit, but swell out of the leaves in the place where fruit would naturally be, suggesting that the woman is herself a tree of life. Her approach to the stream is accompanied by an urgency in the landscape for her to merge totally with it. The water is "impatient" to take her;

the sky floats "solemnly" over her beauty; the river attempts to keep
her "submerged and quiescent," while over her "glories / The Summer." Fusing with nature to become its spirit or life-force, she does
not lose her identity as a woman but expands the significance of
womanhood, becoming a symbol that Lowell discovers and examines:

> Oread, Dryad, or Naiad, or just
> Woman, clad only in youth and in gallant perfection,
> Standing up in a great burst of sunshine, you dazzle my eyes
> Like a snow-star, a moon, your effulgence burns up in a halo,
> For you are the chalice which holds all the races of men.
>
> (C, 223)

The verbal picture has gone beyond sense experience to a mental image, to a sacramental attitude.

The difference between "A Bather" and an early poem like "Teatro
Bambino" is not difficult to see. Besides a more natural language in
"A Bather," its mythological allusion grows organically out of the
poem instead of being forced on it. Similarly, the bather who is the
chalice of the human race is a more substantial and a more symbolic
figure than an earlier and similar portrait of a woman—the fountain
siren of "Clear, with Light Variable Winds."

"A Bather" is typical of Lowell's growing power, but it represents
only one of several kinds of lyrics that she wrote extensively. The imagist influence, which is not strong in "A Bather," is much more pronounced in the shorter haikulike poems that appear in *Pictures of the
Floating World* and *What's O'Clock*. Many of these, although they have
the gemlike hardness and exact language favored by the imagists, ad-
mittedly give little more than surface description—miniature pictures
of trees, leaves, rivers, the sky:

> Circumstance
>
> Upon the maple leaves
> The dew shines red,
> But on the lotus blossom
> It has the pale transparence of tears.
>
> (C, 203)

Others end with an idea or a symbol that their material does not justify, as in "Ombre Chinoise," which is nonetheless a beautiful poem:

Red foxgloves against a yellow wall streaked with plum-coloured shadows;
A lady with a blue and red sunshade;
The slow dash of waves upon a parapet.
That is all.
Non-existent—immortal—
As solid as the centre of a ring of fine gold.

(*C*, 211)[2]

But we must approach even these miniature picture poems with some care, as Foster Damon illustrates in his reading of "Outside a Gate": "On the floor of the empty palanquin / The plum-petals constantly increase" (*C*, 206). It is, as Damon points out, an imagist love poem: "The plum-petals indicate that it is spring; the palanquin is the equipage of a noble; its place at the gate shows that he is visiting; the accumulation of petals shows that his visit is a long one—and to whom does one pay long visits in spring but to one's beloved?"[3] The so-called thinness, that is, of a number of Lowell's lyrics can be more apparent than real, and surface details can signal the presence of underlying emotions or events.

For precise description, with details that are hard and clear and yet suggestive, "Wind and Silver," from *What's O'Clock,* is one of Lowell's best short lyrics and one of the most purely imagistic:

Greatly shining,
The Autumn moon floats in the thin sky;
And the fish-ponds shake their backs and flash their dragon scales
As she passes over them.

(*C*, 477)

The poem suggests a unity in nature, a oneness between sky and earth, moon and pond. The moon "floats," as if it were in water, or as if the ponds were reflected and repeated in the sky. The fish-ponds become fish and assume the denser materiality of animal bodies. But as they "shake their backs and flash their dragon scales," the ponds also take on the property of the moon, reflecting and repeating its light on earth. As we know, the moon is an important symbol in Lowell's poetry, and it is often described in goddesslike terms or as an unattainable enchantress. The metaphorical dragon, on the other hand, evokes the familiar beast from folklore and legend that holds the princess captive or guards the entrance to a magic castle or cave.

Frazer says that dragons are often identified in folktales as water spirits inhabiting and controlling fountains or lakes, and that young women were sometimes sacrificed to them as brides.[4] "Wind and Silver" at least hints at such associations. The moon, a feminine symbol and identified as "she," transforms the ponds into something bestial and alive, a dragon that flashes at her as if to allure or pursue.

And yet the floating moon and the lit ponds have exchanged identities. A similar idea informs "The Sand Altar," which is on the same page as "Wind and Silver" in *The Complete Poetical Works,* and which can be taken as a companion piece to it.

> With a red grain and a blue grain, placed in precisely the proper positions, I made a beautiful god, with plumes of yard-long feathers and a swivel eye.
>
> And with a red grain and a blue grain, placed in precisely the proper positions, I made a dragon, with scaly wings and a curling, iniquitous tail.
>
> Then I reflected:
> If, with the same materials, I can make both god and dragon, of what use is the higher mathematics?
>
> Having said this, I went outdoors and stood under a tree and listened to the frogs singing their evening songs in the green darkness.
>
> (C, 477)

"The Sand Altar" focuses on the very activity that creates a unity of opposites, thus bringing to consciousness the submerged imaginative operations that resulted in the unifying images and metaphors of "Wind and Silver." In both poems, however, the interconnection or common origin of bestial and ideal images questions the dualistic view of the universe as divided between divine and demonic forces. "The Sand Altar," with its moral (as well as mathematical) perplexity, is a more explicit challenge than "Wind and Silver," but neither poem attempts to state a particular philosophy. Rather, Lowell retreats from her discovery that the same materials produce "both god and dragon," back to external nature, to the neighborhood of ponds, as suggested by the frogs. They sing undisturbed, not to a contrasting image of light, but within a green, encompassing darkness.

We do not always find such suggestiveness and depth in Lowell's pictorial lyrics, but for that matter we do not always find them in any poet. The longer written pictures range from the self-conscious word-painting of the poem immediately preceding "A Bather" and aptly named "Impressionist Picture of a Garden":

> Give me sunlight, cupped in a paint brush,
> And smear the red of peonies
> Over my garden.
> Splash blue upon it,
> The hard blue of Canterbury bells . . .
>
> (C, 222)

—where there is little more than an itemization of colors and flowers—to the sexually suggestive, eerie garden in "Sultry":

> To those who can see them, there are eyes,
> Leopard eyes of marigolds crouching above red earth,
> Bulging eyes of fruits and rubies in the heavily-hanging trees,
> Broken eyes of queasy cupids staring from the gloom of myrtles.
> I came here for solitude
> And I am plucked at by a host of eyes.
>
> (C, 469)

The imagery recalls Lowell's earlier poem, "The Basket," in which a woman eats human eyes as calmly as if they were shelled nuts. Here, a garden of eyes threatens to devour a woman. Seeking solitude, she finds herself the focus of a cunning, waiting nature which, with its eyes of leopards and cupids and bulging red fruit, surrounds her with images of fecundity and an intimidating, almost certainly sexual, power.

At the center of the picture, pointing at her, is a statue of Hermes, a god notorious for his amorous interests and called the "ever-smitten Hermes" by Keats in "Lamia." Lowell would surely be aware of the parallel between her poem and the opening scene of Keats's, in which an invisible, shy nymph is revealed to Hermes by a lamia whose body is marked with leopardlike spots and peacock eyes—after which Hermes sexually possesses the nymph. Lowell's Hermes, in a garden where eyes pluck at her and all of nature seems lewdly voyeuristic, is satyrlike and "more savage than the goat-legged Pan." He catches "men's eyes" with his youth, his manhood, and the reticence of [his] everlasting revelation" (*C,* 469). Capturing her attention, Hermes forces Lowell to see, to become "a cunning eye" and thus partake in the sexual character of the garden; and he awakens her imagination, causing her to seek in the distant past for the original Hermes, in an attempt to enter the world or reality of his revelation.

She finds the hidden, original force that this "time-gnawed" statue reveals, but it does not renew her:

> Yours are the eyes of a bull and a panther,
> For all that they are chiselled out and the sockets empty.
> You—perfectly imperfect,
> Clothed in a garden,
> In innumerable gardens,
> Borrowing the eyes of fruits and flowers—
> And mine also, cold, impossible god,
> So that I stare back at myself
> And see myself with loathing.
>
> (*C,* 470)

Having originally gone to the garden to be alone, she now sees herself as others, or as nature and Hermes, see her. The intense self-consciousness of staring at herself results in a self-rejection that recalls her fearful prophesy in "A Fairy Tale," that she would "never . . . be fulfilled by love." But of course "Sultry" is considerably more complex than the early autobiographical poem; Hermes, the object and the cause of sexual awareness, is at once predatory, fruitful, and an empty ruin. And it is not clear whether Lowell's self-hatred results from her admission of her sexual unattractiveness to a Hermes or to any man, or from her rejection of his intimidating and sexually restrictive point of view—a refusal to see herself as a sexual object. Whether the mode of seeing is loathsome, or the woman seen, or both, the experience is destructive, reducing Lowell to a "shadow, tortured out of semblance," who can "see nothing" (*C,* 470). The vivid picture of a garden of eyes ends in sightlessness.

Love Poems: The Lady of her Choice

The single most important figure in Lowell's lyrics is Ada Dwyer Russell, her housemate and companion for the last decade of her life. Dwyer unquestionably gave Lowell emotional ballast and crucial support in the years of controversy and illness that followed 1914. Lowell nicknamed her friend "Peter"—the rock; and she resented and feared

the separations caused by Dwyer's occasional visits to her family.[5]
Whether the two women were physical lovers has not, to my knowledge, been confirmed. Jean Gould refers to, but does not elaborate
upon, Lowell's "bisexual tendencies" and "psychosexual conflict."[6]
Many of Lowell's narratives and monologues, as we have seen, deal
with male-female relations, but the tendency of these is to end in
frustration ("The Cremona Violin," "The Rosebud Wall-Paper"); bitterness ("Patterns"); or psychic or physical destruction ("The Basket,"
"The Great Adventure of Max Breuck"). Of course, conflict, tension,
and even violence are common elements of narrative, and Lowell's
men are as likely to become victims as are her women. Still, just as
there is a great difference between the female-centered, nurturing nature of "A Bather" and Hermes' leering, aggressive garden in "Sultry," so the contrast between the narratives about heterosexual love
and the love lyrics to Ada Dwyer is striking. The Ada Dwyer poems
are marked by tenderness and fulfillment, and often rise to a tone of
rapturous adoration.

As the loved one, Dwyer takes on several roles or identities, which
Lowell develops in some detail in the section of *Pictures of the Floating
World* called "Two Speak Together," a collection of poems dealing
with her and her companion. Dwyer is nature's symbol, a presence
that combines and evokes the beautiful flowers and trees in Lowell's
garden:

> When I think of you, Beloved,
> I see a smooth and stately garden
> With parterres of gold and crimson tulips
> And bursting lilac leaves.
> ("Mise en Scene"; *C*, 210)

In "Wheat-in-the-Ear," where she is a radiant gem, a spear that
burns, Dwyer combines matter and light, form and energy.

> You flash in front of the cedars and the tall spruces,
> And I see that you are fire—
> Sacrificial fire on a jade altar,
> Spear-tongue of white, ceremonial fire.
> (*C*, 211)

She is, in the metaphoric "The Weather-Cock Points South," like an
unblemished white flower from which Lowell carefully peels the
petals.

> One by one
> I parted you from your leaves,
> Until you stood up like a white flower
> Swaying slightly in the evening wind.
>   (C, 211)

Again, but even more explicitly than in "A Bather," a woman's body becomes and takes the place of a plant.

The nakedness in "Wheat-in-the-Ear" and the sensuous, figurative disrobing here recall Lowell's fascination with the nude female body. At the same time, Ada Dwyer was past fifty when the "Two Speak Together" poems appeared, and it is unlikely that Lowell meant the nakedness to be taken literally. Rather, her love for the other woman has stripped their relationship of the patterns that restrain and war against passion; or, to take another idea from "Patterns," Dwyer acts out the desire to become one with nature and to reveal her hidden self. She thus shows Lowell a fresh, ageless beauty. Moreover, an image of a jade cup in "Wheat-in-the-Ear" connects her to the more universal symbol of womanhood in "A Bather"—the "chalice" that "holds" the human race.

Ultimately, Dwyer's nakedness is that of an ideal made flesh, a sacramental revelation of holiness or even divinity in human form, and with very different associations from those of Hermes. In "Mise en Scene," Dwyer's shawl flares behind her like the "draperies of a painted Madonna." Two poems later in the sequence, Dwyer is the "Madonna of the Evening Flowers," at whose feet Lowell longs "to kneel" (C, 210). She is also a modern Venus in "Venus Transiens":

> Tell me,
> Was Venus more beautiful
> Than you are,
> When she topped
> The crinkled waves,
> Drifting shoreward
> On her plaited shell?
>   (C, 210)

By finding in Dwyer the beauty of the Madonna and of a goddess of love, Lowell combines two usually opposed images of woman.

The religious associations suggested by the Madonna and Venus are carried even further and made more explicit. Dwyer—whose beauty inspired Lowell the poet and whose love sustained Lowell the person—becomes a source of sacramental nourishment, the bread and wine of Lowell's life:

> When you came, you were like red wine and honey,
> And the taste of you burnt my mouth with its sweetness.
> Now you are like morning bread,
> Smooth and pleasant.
> I hardly taste you at all for I know your savour,
> But I am completely nourished.
>
> ("A Decade"; C, 217)

Only a letter distinguishes between "savour" and "Saviour," thus strengthening the associations with Christ of the bread and wine. In "Orange of Midsummer," Lowell goes beyond the symbolic bread and wine to blood itself, which Dwyer, like Christ, gives her to drink in a cup—in effect, the chalice, which Lowell identifies with womanhood.

> "Are you thirsty?" said you,
> And held out a cup.
> But the water in the cup was scarlet and crimson
> Like the poppies in your hands.
> "It looks like blood," I said.
> "Like blood," you said,
> "Does it?
> But drink it, my Beloved."
>
> (C, 214)

Not surprisingly, when Ada Dwyer is separated from her, Lowell feels empty and desolate; the nights frighten her, and nature seems meaningless or incomplete, as in "Left Behind":

> I cannot look at the flowers,
> Nor the lifting leaves of the trees.
> Without you, there is no garden,
> No bright colours,
> No shining leaves.
> There is only space,
> Stretching endlessly forward. . . .
>
> (C, 215)

Without Dwyer, a city she is visiting seems "incoherent" and "trivial," and Lowell's "brain aches with emptiness" ("The Sixteenth

Floor"; *C, 215*). In "Autumn," someone brings Lowell a bright yellow dahlia, an image of "Fecundity." But Dwyer's absence makes Lowell barren, and she offers to send the flower to her friend, who has taken with her "All I once possessed" (*C, 215*). With Ada Dwyer gone, the center of the garden, of life, falls apart; without its symbolic flower, its nourishing cup, imagination remains passive before the fecund dahlia. In "Frimaire" (*C, 218*), the last of the "Two Speak Together" poems, Lowell imagines herself and Dwyer as the last two flowers in a late autumn garden, and wonders anxiously about their final separation: which one of them will die first, leaving the other alone? But a haiku, from "The Anniversary" in *What's O'Clock,* states an even closer relationship to her friend, and keeps the flower (and the nourishment) metaphor:

> You wrong me, saying:
> One death will not kill us both.
> Your veins hold my sap.
>
> (*C, 443*)

What's O'Clock also contains the beautiful "Song for a Viola D'Amore," which begins, "The lady of my choice is bright / As a clematis at the touch of night" (*C, 443*), and which is almost certainly an Ada Dwyer poem; and "Vespers," in which Dwyer is again necessary for nature to have meaning. The foxgloves in the poem would burn to her, as to a Venus or Madonna:

> Last night, at sunset,
> The foxgloves were like tall altar candles.
> Could I have lifted you to the roof of the greenhouse, my Dear,
> I should have understood their burning.
>
> (*C, 444*)

"Vespers" is followed by "In Excelsis," the most comprehensive of the Ada Dwyer love poems, the one in which Lowell brings together the various images, symbols, and intimations of the others:

> You—you—
> Your shadow is sunlight on a plate of silver;
> Your footsteps, the seeding-place of lilies;
> Your hands moving, a chime of bells across a windless air.
>
> (*C, 444*)

A profusion of images and details portrays the "you," the loved one, as an encompassing, pervasive force, so that Dwyer's presence—which is like sunlight and water, the sound of bees and wasps, "the perfume of jonquils"—is as close and as vast as that of nature's. As the central figure in the garden, she makes it fruitful—her footsteps are "the seeding place of lilies"; and she feeds, with a sacramental meal, Lowell the gardener: "I drink your lips, / I eat the whiteness of your hands and feet." Though inaccessible as the clouds, the loved one touches the heart mysteriously, like a rainbow. Gould calls "In Excelsis" an "adoration."[7] And in fact, more than anything else, it resembles a modern psalm, a devotional hymn not just to Ada Dwyer, who is not named in any of these poems, but to the redeeming power of love—a human force that virtually takes the place of God and gives meaning and beauty to life, prompting Lowell to respond with "those things" that make her a poet.

But though the lover feels the wonder and power of love, the experience is not the transcendental visitation that came upon the early romantics; nor does Lowell, who once thought of writing a book on Matthew Arnold, seek relief from a Victorian crisis of faith. The experience remains finite, within the familiar world of earth and sky, and the lovers do not have to remain true to each other for protection against a world that is not as true or beautiful as it seemed. Rather, Lowell sings "Glory! Glory!" because Dwyer's presence and love have lit the darkling plain.

Spring and Fall: Intimations of Mortality

In "Frimaire," as already mentioned, Lowell wonders whether she or Ada Dwyer will be the first to die. In "Penumbra," the poem immediately preceding "Frimaire," Lowell thinks of her own death, and wonders what it will be like for Dwyer then. Lowell claims that she will not really be absent, because her house and garden, her pictures and books, which she has known so long and loved so well, will speak to Dwyer for her (*C,* 218). But in "The Garden by Moonlight," Lowell directs her companion to a row of orange lilies. "They knew my mother," she says, "But who belonging to me will they know / When I am gone" (*C,* 212). Despite the high spirits that she showed almost to the end, Lowell thought about mortality more as she grew older and more infirm, and in some of the finest of her later lyrics she took up such issues as the possibilities of permanence in a world governed by change, and explored the connections between time present and time lost.

Two companion poems in *What's O'Clock,* "Lilacs" and "Purple Grackles," juxtapose the two seasons spring and fall, with "Lilacs" celebrating the spring that the flower stands for—"May is lilac here in New England" (*C,* 447)—and "Purple Grackles" memorializing the death of summer as signaled by the birds clustering in the fall. From May in the one poem to September in the other, a season of fulfillment changes into a time portending decay.

"Lilacs" represents the best of the familiar Lowell, the Lowell commonly identified as a word-painter, or imagist turned into an elaborate chronicler of bright surfaces:

> Lilacs,
> False blue,
> White,
> Purple,
> Colour of lilac,
> Your great puffs of flowers
> Are everywhere in this my New England.
>
> (*C,* 446)

But the lilacs provide more than a colorful picture. As the lilacs "are everywhere" now, so they "were everywhere" in the past, thus connecting the present with an earlier New England. Now they watch a deserted house. Earlier, they "tapped the window when the preacher preached his sermon," and "flaunted the fragrance" of their blossoms "Through the wide doors of Custom Houses . . . When a ship was in from China" (*C,* 446). Like sirens of nature, the lilacs tempt the "quill-driving" Custom House clerks until they writhe on their high stools and write poetry "on their letter-sheets behind the propped-up ledgers" (*C,* 446–47). The scene is like a page out of Wordsworth. Quit your books, the lilacs seem to be saying, "May is a month for flitting." But unlike Wordsworth, Lowell makes no claim for a greater moral wisdom in nature. The lilacs simply oppose their beauty to the pursuit of profit, as they stir the restless imaginations of a people devoted to commerce.

Immigrants themselves, moreover, like the New Englanders, the lilacs have spread "From Canada to Narragansett Bay" to become the symbol or emblem of the region's inner self: "You are the great flood of our souls / Bursting above the leaf-shapes of our hearts" (*C,* 447).

Lowell's language makes one body, one being, out of the flowers and the people—the "heart-shaped leaves" of the one matching and mirroring the leaf-shaped "hearts" of the other. The common identity is pressed even closer in the "heart-leaves" of the poem's beautiful final lines:

> Heart-leaves of lilac all over New England,
> Roots of lilac under all the soil of New England,
> Lilacs in me because I am New England,
> Because my roots are in it,
> Because my leaves are of it,
> Because my flowers are for it,
> Because it is my country
> And I speak to it of itself
> And sing of it with my own voice
> Since certainly it is mine.
>
> (C, 447)

As the speaker turns herself into a lilac, thus both personifying the flower and using it as a metaphor for herself, self-discovery and the recognition of a collective, lasting regional identity take place together.

In *What's O'Clock*, "Lilacs" is immediately followed by "Purple Grackles," and as the season changes from May to September, so does the color of the landscape to the darker purple and black of the grackles. Unlike the deep-rooted, permanent lilacs, moreover, the grackles are only temporary visitors, stopping each year for a short stay in Lowell's garden on their migration south. Their sudden appearance startles and delights her, and though its meaning is essentially somber, the poem opens with an amused, celebratory welcoming of the birds:

> The grackles have come.
> The smoothness of the morning is puckered with their incessant chatter.
> A sociable lot, these purple grackles,
> Thousands of them strung across a long run of wind,
> Thousands of them beating the air-ways with quick wing-jerks,
> Spinning down the currents of the South.
>
> (C, 447)

Her attitude even becomes whimsical as Lowell wonders if the grackles are perhaps really blackberries, they cluster in the trees so thickly, or like highwaymen and thieves, except that they are so loud and unstealthy. Only when she realizes that they are stealing her summer does a different note enter, for the dark birds force her to see that her "hydrangea blooms are rusty," that the golden hearts of the flowers are changing to "lusterless seeds," and that the sun is as pale as a shrinking lemon. She "did not see this yesterday, / But to-day the grackles have come" (C, 448).

Though the seasonal changes are taking place as close to Lowell as her own garden, and though the grackles envelop her, she does not become one with them or their world as she did with the lilacs. Even when the antics of the birds delight her, as when they use her rain-filled gutter for bathing because she has not provided them with a suitable bath, her language suggests that she remains indoors, watching them from behind the safety of her window. She speaks of herself as their host, but knows that they do not take her into account or consider her important:

Tyrian-feathered freebooter,
Appropriating my delightful gutter with so extravagant an ease,
You are as cool a pirate as ever scuttled a ship,
And are you not scuttling my Summer with every peck of your sharp bill?
(C, 448)

It is an amusing, even a touching scene, and the one in which Lowell comes closest to the foreign, animal independence of the grackles—to the otherness of nature. She addresses the bird, as she repeatedly did the lilacs, with the conversational "you." Elsewhere in the poem she uses the more distant and impersonal "they." But Lowell can come this close to the grackles because her window separates her from them; and the scene as a whole, an incident in the "scuttling" of her summer, underscores her helplessness as a human to do anything about the changes that nature brings.

While she can "only stare stupidly out of the window," the grackles depart as suddenly and mysteriously as they arrived, "and it is a year gone by":

And I watch an Autumn storm
Stripping the garden,
Shouting black rain challenges
To an old, limp Summer
Laid down to die in the flower-beds.
(C, 449)

Tragedy has evolved out of whimsical, comic beginnings, as a world full of movement and sound becomes old and limp, and as a deadly black rain replaces the lively black birds. The world of "Lilacs" seems far removed, yet its companion poem mourns for the world that poem celebrated.

Taken together, "Lilacs" and "Purple Grackles" encompass the spring and fall of external nature. "On Looking at a Copy of Alice Meynell's Poems" moves the cycle inward to the soul's experiences of youth and age, past and present. Lowell's friend Frances Dabney had given her the volume of Meynell's poems in the late 1890s, while the two of them were in Devonshire, England, where Lowell hoped to shake off a severe nervous depression. Reading the book again, after Meynell's death in 1922, Lowell recalls that earlier painful time when she and Dabney read it first:

> You gave this book to me to ease
> The smart in me you could not heal.
> Your gift a mirror—woe or weal.
> We sat beneath the apple-trees.
>
> And I remember how they rang,
> These words, like bronze cathedral bells
> Down ancient lawns, or citadels
> Thundering with gongs where choirs sang.
>
> Silent the sea, the earth, the sky,
> And in my heart a silent weeping.
> Who has not sown can know no reaping!
> Bitter conclusion and no lie.
>
> O heart that sorrows, heart that bleeds,
> Heart that was never mine, your words
> Were like the pecking Autumn birds
> Stealing away my garnered seeds.
>
> No future where there is no past!
> O cherishing grief which laid me bare,
> I wrapped you like a wintry air
> About me. Poor enthusiast!

> (C, 537)

Lowell remembers her early womanhood, not as the traditional springtime of youth, but as a barren, bitter season. The Meynell poems, in which she sees herself as in a "mirror," are like a "wintry air," or "Autumn birds" stealing the last of her pent-up, unfruitful feelings. The silent, almost colorless landscape of the beginning of the poem also mirrors, and is made the projection of, her silent suffering, while a ship that "sleeps" motionlessly for three hours symbolizes the inertia of her feelings, the state she is stuck in. Yet while the landscape portrays her, her condition remains invisible to her friend. Instead of intimacy and sharing between the two women, there is separation and blindness. Lowell remembers Dabney with kindness, but a harsh accusation—were you made of "wood or stone?"—reveals her essential loneliness, her sense of being in the company of a stranger instead of a friend. Even Meynell's poems, in which Lowell finds a fellow sufferer in a stranger, seem distant and of another time, like cathedral bells over "ancient lawns" or thunderings in empty choir lofts—with Lowell's image echoing Shakespeare's powerful metaphor for the autum of life: "those boughs which shake against the cold / Bare ruin'd choirs, where late the sweet birds sang."[8] Lowell's fear, moreover, in what should be the springtime of her life, is that she will have no harvest, will "know no reaping." In 1899 she had not yet discovered the outlet of poetry, but rather finds her feelings appropriated and expressed in the verses of another. In more than one sense of the term, then, she has come to a "Bitter conclusion."

The last stanzas of the poem return to the present. The episode seems "strange" in 1922, when Lowell can remember but is no longer possessed by the griefs of 1899. Meynell's poems do not move her as they did, or ring like bells, but are simply well-crafted lines fading into the past they belong to: "The ink is pale, the letters fade. / The verses seem to be well made" (C, 537). Reminding her that the time that they mirrored is dead, they lead her to think of death—first Dabney's, then Meynell's:

> And you are dead these drifted years,
> How many I forget. And she
> Who wrote the book, her tragedy
> Long since dried up its scalding tears.

> I read of her death yesterday,
> Frail lady whom I never knew
> And knew so well. Would I could strew
> Her grave with pansies, blue and grey.

Would I could stand a little space
Under a blowing, brightening sky,
And watch the sad leaves fall and lie
Gently upon that lonely place.

So cried her heart, a feverish thing.
But clay is still, and clay is cold,
And I was young, and I am old,
And in December what birds sing!

(C, 537)

In effect, the poem portrays a spiritual wasteland, the soul's encounter with desolate or destructive truths. Though the present has moved beyond the past, there is little indication of a change for the better in the quarter century since Lowell first read Meynell. If anything, as the last surviver of the trio in the poem, her loneliness is even more complete. Time brings death, not renewal, and the autumn landscape remains or edges closer to winter, when the autumn of harvesting birds changes into birdless December. Like the motionless ship, like Lowell's old nervous prostration, the seasonal cycle gets stuck and breaks down.

Thus, the *In Memoriam* stanza that Lowell had used in one of her earliest poems is particularly appropriate for this, one of her last. For "On Looking at a Copy of Alice Meynell's Poems" is a memorial to all three of the women in it: to the well-meaning but imperceptive friend who became a stranger, to the poet whose tragedy has long since cooled, and to the earlier self from whom Lowell is as separated now as she is from the other two. Not only have past emotions and relationships died, they have left little trace in the present; their having been brings little comfort. Hence, Lowell does not recall the past to keep it in memory, but to have done with it:

Go, wistful book, go back again
Upon your shelf and gather dust.
I've seen the glitter through the rust
Of old, long years, I've known the pain.

I've recollected both of you,
But I shall recollect no more.
Between us I must shut the door.
The living have so much to do.

(C, 537)

Perhaps not all is dark in this essentially dark and troubled poem, which is itself a hard-won harvest of the past, despite Lowell's fear that she would know no reaping of her old suffering. The distant emotions still glitter through the rust of time, even if they can no longer be felt. And she looks ahead to the business of living. But even here, Lowell speaks with more resignation than eagerness or sense of triumph over mortality, in a tone not unlike that of Hopkins when, in another poem about isolation and hoarded pain, he called himself "a lonely began."[9]

The "Alice Meynell" poem is powerful in its very negations—its sense of helplessness, loss, and the corroding, killing years. A sonnet to Eleanora Duse, one of six written at about the same time as "Alice Meynell," deals just as honestly with similar ideas, but celebrates the power of a soul to survive the years and even grow more luminous as mortality approaches:

> Seeing you stand once more before my eyes
> In your pale dignity and tenderness,
> Wearing your frailty like a misty dress
> Draped over the great glamour which denies
> To years their domination, all disguise
> Time can achieve is but to add a stress,
> A finer fineness, as though some caress
> Touched you a moment to a strange surprise.
>   (C, 480)

Lowell had not seen Duse since 1902, when she was inspired by the actress to write her first poem. Now, in 1923, Duse was sixty-five years old, gaunt, white haired, and, like Lowell, near death. But in the sonnet, the frail body is only an outward, almost transparent dress, through which Lowell can see and affirm something that is permanent or eternal, so that "after these long lengths of years . . . the glory come[s] again"—thus uniting past and present as one time. Duse, though not idealized as a Madonna or a Venus, but merely human, becomes Lowell's symbol of man's victory over time. Though the body ages, it is not vanquished by time, but becomes more spiritual. And all time can do to the soul is give a finer edge to its power to transcend time.

In what G. R. Ruihley aptly calls "those superb images of renewal and healing in the concluding lines of the poem,"[10] Lowell extends the power to defeat time into nature, making it a natural principle or force—in the sun that shines through shafts of rain; in the moon, Lowell's familiar symbol of transcendent beauty, lighting up a sick man's bed; in the daffodils, flowers of spring, growing in a waste of leaves. Images of spring and fall, the promising and the perishing, appear together in a beautifully written traditional sonnet in which Lowell uses the precision and natural speech of the New Poetry. And like most of Lowell's best work, it is faithful to the appearance and inquiring into the mysteries of life.

Chapter Seven
Conclusion

At her death in 1925, Amy Lowell was unquestionably one of the best known and most controversial figures in American poetry. To many, it must have seemed that if the preceding decade belonged to anybody, it belonged to her. Her books sold well and had been widely reviewed. Her poems, essays, and reviews had appeared in numerous journals, and as a popular reader she probably stirred more interest in poetry than anyone else of her time. On 2 March 1925, *Time* magazine featured her on its cover and called her a "renowned" critic and poet. In a sympathetic obituary-editorial, the *New York Times* called her work "stimulating and vivid."[1] When Lowell died, Ferris Greenslet, her editor at Houghton Mifflin, felt "as if a force of nature had been turned off."[2] Most of her contemporaries felt that her campaign for the New Poetry had made its formative years a far more vital period than they would otherwise have been. "No poet living in America," Louis Untermeyer wrote in 1919, "has been more fought for, fought against, and generally fought about than Amy Lowell."[3]

Today, no one thinks of 1914–25 as the age of Lowell. She has almost—not entirely of course—disappeared from discussions of the era she largely dominated and helped to shape. "Patterns" and perhaps half a dozen other of her poems occasionally appear in text books and anthologies, but she is not included, for instance, in the influential *Norton Anthology of Modern Poetry*. Her individual volumes, so handsomely designed, which once made so much traffic in the literary marketplace, have become mere collector's items, and critics are largely silent about the poems that once raised more than one storm.

Lowell's decline in reputation began shortly after her death, although interest in her as a flamboyant personality remained high and still persists. In 1935 Winfield Townley Scott estimated that Lowell was being mentioned in print on an average of three times every day. But Scott later remembered an editor saying to him in 1935, " 'Who the hell . . . wants to read about Amy Lowell?' "[4] *PMLA* bibliographies from 1931 to 1951 list only five Lowell items, not one of which is primarily critical. For Untermeyer, Lowell's poetry lost its vitality as soon as Lowell was no longer around to read it. The "blood went out of it," he claims, after her death. "The color seemed superficially applied, the warmth simulated; with the exception of some seven or eight poems, the verse was suddenly lifeless."[5] Whereas in 1919 Untermeyer had praised Lowell as "our most radical innovator" and "the most versatile woman that has ever written poetry in America," in 1939 he finds little about her work that is even worth discussing: "Amy too often wrote to fit a theory, to mold her work in the fashion of the moment; she cast herself in the role of public poet. Instead of being urged by the quiet subconscious self, she continually prodded the conscious will. She sacrificed a slow searching for quick brilliance, and exchanged a broad understanding for narrow contemporaneousness. Her amazing range of subjects and variety of techniques . . . no longer hide the central poverty."[6] This difference in opinion, from one who was close to Lowell, almost defies understanding. Was our most radical innovator concealing all the time a superficial opportunism? Or has Untermeyer himself sacrificed a slow searching for truth to gain quick brilliance and contemporary approval?

Perhaps it was inevitable that the excessive praise Lowell often received during her life would change into an equally distorted disparagement of her work after her death—and of course other writers have suffered abrupt and drastic reversals on the literary wheel of fortune. Yet there are other factors at work in the obscuring of Lowell's achievement. Whether or not Ruihley is right to blame the new critics for being influenced by Eliot and Pound against Lowell, thus leading to her exclusion from anthologies, there is no question that Lowell made enemies.[7] She was abrasive and dogmatic. Wanting to believe in her own importance, yet bothered by deep self-doubts, she took criticism badly and was scornful of most academic scholars, whom she persistently regarded as enemies of poetry. One repeatedly reads of her summoning editors and dictating terms to them. Despite her sense of poets belonging to one family, she was very competitive, and often thought of other poets as adversaries, against whom she did not always fight fairly. And she was a fat, rich woman who too often patronized people or pushed them around. She became, after all, a legend in her own time, and the legend still has vitality and notoriety. If, as was often the case, her colorful idiosyncrasies blinded her admirers to the real defects in her work, it is not rash to assume that her less attractive qualities caused others to focus on her egotism and to undervalue or completely ignore her work.

But Lowell's personality and the possible prejudices of a critical school do not entirely account for her obscurity today, however they may have operated in the past. The fact is that Lowell could be incredibly wrong about her contemporaries and the future of poetry, as when she denied that *The Waste Land* was poetry. She was a poor critic of her own verse, sometimes boosting as "the best poem I have written" a work of very questionable value; and she published too many inferior and wordy poems. She wrote a clear, readable prose, but she was not a great or systematic thinker. Try as she did to establish an objective basis for free verse, she could only, as F. Cudworth Flint observes, "overstate" preconceived opinions:

> She declares that the laws governing free-verse cadences are "absolute" and "mathematical." Yet nowhere does she provide any definitions of these laws, any criteria with respect to which absoluteness might be established. Unless indeed her discussion amounts to saying that such cadences must absolutely accord with the taste of the poet who devises them—and this individualistic kind of absoluteness, being perceptible only to God and the poet, is no absoluteness at all for the poet's audience. As for the "mathematical" laws, neither in phrase nor in formula are these ever disclosed.[8]

In fact, Lowell did attempt to provide a mathematical formula for the interval between accents in a set of free-verse lines; but Flint is substantially correct. And Lowell's experiments with Professor Patterson did not, to my knowledge, ever lead to anything.

But if Lowell was not as great a poet as she and some of her first admirers thought she was, it does not mean that she was no poet at all. Nor does it follow that she had nothing to say because she often concentrated on the sensory qualities of objects and scenes. She surely wrote more than the seven or eight significant poems usually allotted her. Horace Gregory hardly grants her even that much. For him, Lowell's *Complete Poetical Works* "is a sad book, a lifeless monument to ten years of industry in jotting observations down on paper"—and, in what is probably the low point in Lowell's posthumous fame, he predicts that if she achieves an immortality, it will be in the letters Lawrence wrote to her.[9] More recently, there have been signs that Lowell is beginning to recover some of the critical ground she lost. Ruihley has come to her defense. Feminist critics have begun to notice her. And in 1980 C. David Heymann offered a very different estimate of her worth than Gregory's. "Amy's achievement," Heymann says, "cannot be fully appreciated unless one realizes how the terror and despair that constantly assailed her were overcome in poems which, although fully in touch with human anguish, often succeeded in spite of their dark and forbidding nature. Amy's poems explore those shadowy depths of man's condition with an understanding that in the end affirms our presence, reaffirms our hard-won existence. The final note of so many volumes of her work is not madness or death but simply Amy's exhilaration, her faith."[10]

That is high praise. But if Heymann in 1980 differs with Gregory in 1958, as much as Untermeyer differed with himself over an earlier twenty-year span, the three critics have one important thing in common. Like many others who have written about Lowell—and the exceptions, such as Ruihley, are notable—they do not critically examine her work. Instead of detailed analysis of how well or how badly she wrote, they tend to offer unexamined assumptions about her superficiality or, in Heymann's case, her depth. Perhaps we have not fully learned how to read this "public" poet who does not require the scholarly apparatus needed for an Eliot; who wanders among so many different themes, forms, styles, and rhythms; and who does not stick to a readily identifiable voice. "Sea-Blue and Blood-Red," "Written on the Reverse," "The Rosebud Wall-Paper," "Taxi," "The Green Bowl," "Lilacs," the Eleanora Duse or the Ada Dwyer poems—only a professional at her craft could attempt, let alone execute, such various work. But that so few of her good poems are generally known at all is almost certainly due to the fact that too many of her readers have been content to make generalizations about her poetry instead of engaging it critically.

I have tried to show that there is a great deal in Lowell's poetry worth exploring and discussing. She became an accomplished story-teller, and she knew enough about human nature to create such complex characters as those in "The Doll" and "Written on the Reverse." In telling of a fox's infatuation with the moon, or Perry's journey to Japan, she could make her images and symbols both subtle and resonant. In her best lyrics, she paid the same attention to the impact of words, and drew upon their symbolic and connotative possibilities. She was as adept an artist with the figurative colors of her language as she was a word-painter. But even in those poems in which there is no more than what meets the eye, there is much to see; and we have just begun to get to the core of the best of the others. With her amazing diversity, her different experiments, her obtuseness at one moment and her clearheadedness at another, and her many failures and successes, she is not an easy poet to sum up—which makes many of the still prevailing assumptions about her all the more suspect. This much seems sure: she contributed not a little to the age of Yeats, Pound, and Eliot; and it would have been a very different and less exciting time without her.

Notes and References

Chapter One

1. "The Poetry Bookshop," *Little Review* 2 (May 1915):19.
2. Elizabeth Sergeant, *Fire Under the Andes* (New York, 1927), 19, 30.
3. Louis Untermeyer, *From Another World: The Autobiography of Louis Untermeyer* (New York, 1939), 102.
4. Ferris Greenslet, *The Lowells and Their Seven Worlds* (Boston, 1946), 379.
5. "That Bookcase," *New York Evening Post,* 18 September 1920, Literary Review sec., p. 1.
6. "Early Years of the Saturday Club," *New York Times,* 23 March 1919, 148.
7. Elizabeth Ward Perkins, "Amy Lowell of New England," *Scribner's Magazine* 82 (September 1927):335.
8. Mrs. William Lowell Putnam, "A Glimpse of Amy Lowell's Childhood by her Sister," manuscript quoted by S. Foster Damon, *Amy Lowell: A Chronicle,* (Boston, 1935), 39.
9. Perkins, "Amy Lowell," 329.
10. Damon, *Amy Lowell,* 65, 89.
11. Ibid., 50–54, 66. Damon reprints "What Made Willy Bright Like to Go to Bed" on 76–82.
12. "That Bookcase," 2.
13. Damon, *Amy Lowell,* 90, 92, 93 (quoting from Lowell's diary).
14. Ibid., 90.
15. *Tendencies in Modern American Poetry* (New York, 1917), 250; hereafter cited in the text as *T.*
16. Lowell to Archibald MacLeish, 16 October 1924; Amy Lowell Collection, Harvard University.
17. "That Bookcase," 2.
18. Richard Aldington, *Life for Life's Sake: A Book of Reminiscences* (New York, 1941), 137; and F. S. Flint, "Six French Poets," *Egoist* 3 (January 1916):10.
19. Damon, *Amy Lowell,* 119–20. Jean Gould suggests that the errant suitor may not have existed. See *Amy: The World of Amy Lowell and the Imagist Movement* (New York, 1975), 65.
20. "Poetry, Imagination, and Education," in *Poetry and Poets: Essays by Amy Lowell* (Boston, 1930), 53–54. The essay first appeared in 1917.

21. Leigh Hunt, *Imagination and Fancy: Or Selections from the English Poets* (London: Smith, Elder & Co., 1844), 49–50.

22. The letter is quoted by Eunice Tietjens in "Apologia," *Poetry: A Magazine of Verse* 22 (August 1923):271–72.

23. *The Complete Poetical Works of Amy Lowell*, Intro. Louis Untermeyer (Boston, 1955), 593; hereafter cited in the text as *C*. A series of sonnets, written much later, is given the same title as this first poem.

24. Damon, *Amy Lowell*, 182–83. I will refer to Ada Dwyer by her maiden (and stage) name, rather than by her married name.

25. Gould, *Amy*, 152. Gould is very good on Ada Dwyer's personality and background, and on her importance to Lowell.

26. Damon, *Amy Lowell*, 186.

27. *Letters of Vachel Lindsay*, ed. Marc Chénetier (New York: Burt Franklin & Co., 1979), 455.

28. Damon, *Amy Lowell*, 196.

29. Ezra Pound, "A Few Don'ts by an Imagiste," *Poetry: A Magazine of Verse* 1 (March 1913):202. Damon (*Amy Lowell*, 197–208) discusses the early history of imagism. For more detailed studies, see Glenn Hughes, *Imagism and the Imagists: A Study in Modern Poetry* (Stanford, 1931), 11 ff.; and Stanley K. Coffman, Jr., *Imagism: A Chapter for the History of Modern Poetry* (Norman, Okla. 1951), 3–46.

30. John Gould Fletcher, *Life Is My Song: The Autobiography of John Gould Fletcher* (New York, 1937), 87, 88. Fletcher provides a detailed account of Lowell's trips to London in 1913 and 1914.

31. Ibid., 103–4.

32. Lowell's letter is quoted by Harriet Monroe in *A Poet's Life* (New York, 1938), 276–77.

33. Fletcher, *Life Is My Song*, 145.

34. These details of Lowell's imagist dinner are given by Fletcher, in ibid., 148–51.

35. *The Letters of Ezra Pound, 1907–1941*, ed. D. D. Paige (New York: Harcourt, Brace & Co., 1950), 38, 39.

36. Aldington, *Life for Life's Sake*, 139–40.

37. Damon, *Amy Lowell*, 237–40.

38. *The Letters of Ezra Pound*, 48.

39. Ibid., 43–44.

40. Ibid., 44.

41. See Lowell to Pound, 3 November 1914; in Damon, *Amy Lowell*, 274–75.

42. Preface to *Some Imagist Poets: An Anthology* (Boston: Houghton Mifflin., 1915), viii.

43. Damon, *Amy Lowell*, 304.

44. *The Letters of Ezra Pound*, 121, 122.

45. Monroe, *A Poet's Life*, 277; and Damon, *Amy Lowell*, 311.

46. *The Complete Poetical Works of Amy Lowell,* 145.

47. Jean Starr Untermeyer, *Private Collection* (New York, 1965), 75; and—another eyewitness—Jessie B. Rittenhouse, *My House of Life: An Autobiography* (Boston, 1934), 256–58.

48. Damon, *Amy Lowell,* 393.

49. Ibid., 602.

50. For a good account of Lowell's attempts to gain more notice from Monroe, see Ellen Williams, *Harriet Monroe and the Poetry Renaissance* (Urbana, 1977), 130–45.

51. Margaret Anderson, *My Thirty Years War* (New York: Covici, Friede, 1930), 61–62.

52. Damon, *Amy Lowell,* 467.

53. Ibid., 426.

54. Ibid., 436–37.

55. Ibid., 477; also see 366, 385, 521.

56. Ibid., 535.

57. Ibid., 604. Gould (*Amy,* 318–19) quotes from the same letter, but says that it was written to Elizabeth Sergeant. Frost and Lindsay did, in fact, feel some resentment toward Lowell.

58. The history of this often amusing episode is given by William Jay Smith, *The Spectra Hoax* (Middletown, Conn.: Wesleyan University Press, 1961). Lowell was suspicious of the spectrists, but she was later fooled by a similar hoax perpetrated by Malcolm Cowley and Foster Damon. See ibid., 47–53.

59. Harley Farnsworth MacNair, ed., *Florence Ayscough and Amy Lowell: Correspondence of a Friendship* (Chicago, 1945), 184.

60. See "Mr. Fletcher's Verse," *New Republic* 3 (15 May 1915):49; and Damon, *Amy Lowell,* 291–92.

61. George Lane, "Some Imagist Poets," *Little Review* 2 (May 1915):27–35. In his bibliography of Lowell's works, Damon attributes this essay to Lowell and Fletcher (*Amy Lowell,* 731); but he does not discuss it in his text. Not only are the opinions of the essay the same as Lowell's, but its prose style is very similar to hers. George Lane writes, "Long poems require a different technique from short poems, and perhaps Mr. Aldington has not yet become master of it" (29). Three months later, a restatement of that idea appeared in an article on Aldington signed by Lowell: "He must study the requirements of the longer poem a little more before he will be quite at home in it." See "Richard Aldington's Poetry," *Little Review* 2 (September 1915):15. While there are other explanations for the similarity, Lowell did often repeat material from her earlier essays.

62. Untermeyer, *Private Collection,* 80–81. I have taken the date from Gould, *Amy,* 272.

63. "Walt Whitman and the New Poetry," in *Poetry and Poets,* 63.

64. Lowell to Carl Sandburg, 25 November 1919; Amy Lowell Col-

lection, Harvard University. The Whitman debate is fully described by Damon, *Amy Lowell,* 515–19; I have also used the accounts of it from the *Philadelphia Public Ledger,* 13–14 November 1919.

65. Gould, *Amy,* 284. Damon only says that on 11 November A. Edward Newton was to give Lowell a dinner "but had to cancel it on account of a heart attack" (*Amy Lowell,* 514)—which suggests that Newton, not Lowell, suffered the attack. It is hard to believe that Lowell would have attended the Centenary the day after a heart attack. Gould does not cite her source of information.

66. Gould, *Amy,* 204. The story is a favorite among writers on Lowell.

67. Ibid., 324.

68. Lowell hoped to use *Fir-Flower Tablets* to get an advantage over Pound. See Donald A. Precosky, " 'Make Ezra Pound and the Whole Caboodle of Them Sit Up': Florence Ayscough and the Lowell-Pound Feud," *Four Decades of Poetry, 1890–1930* 2 (July 1979):204–9.

69. Hyder Edward Rollins and Stephen Maxfield Parrish, *Keats and the Bostonians* (Cambridge, Mass., 1951), 107–8. The information about her Keats collection is given in a letter by Lowell to Ferris Greenslet.

70. Ibid., 111, 87.

71. Ibid., 175.

72. Damon, *Amy Lowell,* 666–67.

73. Eleanor Robson Belmont, *The Fabric of Memory* (New York, 1957), 199.

74. Damon, *Amy Lowell,* 699–701.

75. Sergeant, *Fire Under the Andes,* 29.

76. Harriet Monroe, "Memories of Amy Lowell," in *Poets and Their Art* (New York, 1926), 251.

Chapter Two

1. "Is There a National Spirit in 'The New Poetry' of America?" *Craftsman* 30 (July 1916):340; hereafter cited in the text as *I*.

2. *Six French Poets* (New York, 1915), 15, 125; hereafter cited in the text as *Si*.

3. Harriet Monroe, "Miss Lowell on Tendencies," *Poetry: A Magazine of Verse* 11 (December 1917):152–53.

4. F. S. Flint, "Imagisme," and Ezra Pound, "A Few Don'ts by an Imagiste," *Poetry: A Magazine of Verse* 1 (March 1913):198–206. Lowell summarizes the imagist platform in *Tendencies,* 235–46.

5. Conrad Aiken, "The Place of Imagism," *New Republic* 3 (22 May 1915):75–76; and Harold Monro, "The Imagists Discussed," *Egoist* 2 (May 1915):77–80. Both articles raised cogent objections to imagism.

6. Aiken, "Place of Imagism," 75. Aiken does not name or cite the poem that was printed backward.

7. Monro, "Imagists Discussed," 78, 79, 80.

8. "A Consideration of Modern Poetry," *North American Review* 205 (January 1917):104–6; hereafter cited in the text as *Co*.

9. "The New Manner in Modern Poetry," *New Republic* 6 (4 March 1916):125; hereafter cited in the text as *N*.

10. See Harry T. Moore, *The Intelligent Heart: The Story of D. H. Lawrence* (Harmondsworth, England: Penguin Books, 1960), 227.

11. Fletcher, *Life Is My Song*, 92–93. Fletcher did not like the phrase "the unrelated method"; and it did lead to misunderstandings.

12. "Some Musical Analogies in Modern Poetry," *Musical Quarterly* 6 (January 1920):135; hereafter cited in the text as *S*.

13. Quoted by Damon, *Amy Lowell*, 339.

14. "Emily Dickinson," in *Poetry and Poets*, 88–108.

15. "*Vers Libre* and Metrical Prose," *Poetry: A Magazine of Verse* 3 (March 1914):216.

16. Preface to *Some Imagist Poets, 1916* (Boston: Houghton Mifflin Co., 1916), ix–x. Although the preface is not signed, it was almost certainly written, entirely or substantially, by Lowell.

17. See "Some Musical Analogies," 148. There are parallels that I do not believe have been explored, between Lowell's approach to poetic rhythm through music and that of Gerard Manley Hopkins.

18. For more detail on the Lowell-Patterson experiments, see Lowell's "The Rhythms of Free Verse," *Dial* 64 (17 January 1918):51–56; and William Morrison Patterson, "New Verse and New Prose," *North American Review* 207 (February 1918):257–67.

19. "Poetry as a Spoken Art," in *Poetry and Poets*, 14–15.

20. Lowell's debt to Fort is fully discussed in René Taupin, *L'Influence du Symbolisme Francais sur La Poésie Américaine (de 1910 a 1920)* (Paris, 1929), 180–92.

21. Damon, *Amy Lowell*, 257.

22. John Livingstone Lowes, *Convention and Revolt in Poetry* (Boston: Houghton Mifflin Co., 1919), 288.

23. Aldington, *Life For Life's Sake*, 141–42.

24. "Poetry, Imagination, and Education," in *Poetry and Poets*, 55; and see 29–30, 34, 43–44.

Chapter Three

1. Quoted in Damon, *Amy Lowell*, 278.

2. See William C. Bedford, "A Musical Apprentice: Amy Lowell to Carl Engel," *Musical Quarterly* 58 (October 1972):527.

3. From "New York at Night," in *Complete Poetical Works*, 12.

4. "Is There a National Spirit in 'The New Poetry' of America?" *Craftsman* 30 (July 1916):346.

5. Damon, *Amy Lowell*, 151. Damon gives the 1903 date for the poem.

6. "Adonais" is included in most editions of Shelley. The passage quoted is st. 52, ll. 460–64.

7. As Damon notes, *Sword Blades and Poppy Seed* "made quite a stir" (*Amy Lowell*, 260); and it was widely, though not always enthusiastically, reviewed. For Louis Untermeyer, Lowell's first two books are worlds apart. Nothing in *Dome* anticipated the new and surprising work in *Sword Blades and Poppy Seed*. See *The New Era in American Poetry* (New York, 1919), 140–41.

8. Lowell claimed this in her preface to *Sword Blades and Poppy Seed* (New York, 1914), xii.

9. Damon, *Amy Lowell*, 258.

10. In *Amy*, Jean Gould observes that "probably no other woman poet of her time described the female nude body as often or as sensuously as Amy Lowell" (181).

Chapter Four

1. Preface to *Men, Women and Ghosts* (New York, 1916), vii.

2. Cf. Janet Overmeyer, "Which Broken Pattern?—A Note on Amy Lowell's 'Patterns,' " *Notes on Contemporary Literature*, 1, no. 3 (May 1971):14–15. Overmeyer argues that the fiancé has proposed a natural, rather than a legal, marriage to the woman, and that she has accepted it.

3. My allusion is to the well-known statement by Keats in a letter to Benjamin Bailey, on 22 November 1817: "The Imagination may be compared to Adam's dream—he awoke and found it truth." Lowell owned the letter and quotes the "Adam's dream" section of it in her *John Keats* (Boston, 1925), 1:526.

4. Archibald MacLeish considered "Pickthorn Manor" the most successful poem in *Men, Women and Ghosts*, and notes that the story "turns upon . . . a confusion of personalities due to emotional association" ("Amy Lowell and the Art of Poetry," *North American Review* 221 [March 1925]:516).

5. Lowell's attitude toward Charlotta, as expressed in a letter to Winifred Bryher on 29 June 1918, is more severe than mine. She criticizes Charlotta for accusing her husband of neglecting her, when in fact he does love her, but as an artist has a more important commitment to his music: "she was too selfish to be the wife of an artist, although she had enough artistic feeling to be attracted and held by this very art, which, in the final count, she was so terribly jealous of" (quoted in Damon, *Amy Lowell*, 377).

6. James Frazer lists a number of such dismemberment myths. See James George Frazer, *The New Golden Bough,* ed. Dr. Theodor H. Gaster (New York: Mentor Books, 1964), 406–8.

7. The Whitman references, almost certainly familiar to Lowell, are from sections 1 and 6 of "Song of Myself."

8. There are several parallels between Amos Sears and Heathcliff, besides the intensity of their attachment to and grief over a woman. Both are nonnatives to the place they grow up in; both leave their homes for a time; both have wives who desert them; both are essentially loners who reject conventional religion.

9. Some of the sources for the stories in *East Wind* are given in Damon, *Amy Lowell,* 711–12. A number of the poems from *East Wind,* as from her other two posthumous books, were published earlier by Lowell in various journals. "The Doll" first appeared in 1921.

10. Preface to *Men, Women and Ghosts,* x.

11. Ibid., vii.

12. Damon discusses the *Phantasms of War* poems and Lowell's attitude toward poetry as propaganda (see *Amy Lowell,* 717–23).

Chapter Five

1. Preface to *Can Grande's Castle* (New York, 1918), ix, vii.

2. Preface to *Legends* (Boston, 1921), v–vi.

3. James Tupper, "The Poetry of Amy Lowell," *Sewanee Review* 28 (January 1920):52.

4. Conrad Aiken, "The Technique of Polyphonic Prose: Amy Lowell," in *Scepticisms: Notes on Contemporary Poetry* (Freeport, N.Y., 1967), 122–23. More recently, F. Cudworth Flint experienced a similar feeling of "exhausted stupefaction" after reading *Can Grande's Castle.* See *Amy Lowell* (Minneapolis, 1969), 30.

5. As we saw in chapter 2, Lowell defended the externalist use of images for themselves, and argued against the notion that they should have metaphorical, human significance. This is clearly not the case with the images in *Can Grande's Castle* or with many of her imagist poems. Her quarrel, in effect, was with a poetry that used images didactically or editorially.

6. Lowell's explanation of the final scenes is different. She wanted to show, she said, how the Japanese mind broke down in its effort to assimilate Western thought. See Damon, *Amy Lowell,* 475.

7. See the preface to *Can Grande's Castle,* xiv; and Robert T. Self, "The Correspondence of Amy Lowell and Barrett Wendell, 1915–1919," *New England Quarterly* 47 (March 1974):79–80. Wendell warned Lowell about her overuse of rhyme.

8. Aiken, "Technique of Polyphonic Prose," 124. The passage can be found in the *Complete Poetical Works,* 185.

9. Aiken, p. 123. Percy H. Boynton also objected to the "immensely self-conscious" nature of Lowell's polyphonic prose, in "Amy Lowell," in *Some Contemporary Americans: The Personal Equation in Literature* (Chicago, 1924), 81. Archibald MacLeish, on the other hand, praised *Can Grande's Castle* as a new epic form, claiming that "if it is not the greatest invention of an American, American art has pinnacles we have not suspected." See "Amy Lowell and the Art of Poetry," *North American Review* 221 (March 1925):518.

10. Preface to *Legends*, vii.

11. Ibid., vi.

12. I used Robert Burton, *The Anatomy of Melancholy*, ed. Floyd Dell and Paul Jordan-Smith (New York: Farrar & Rinehart, 1927), p. 649.

13. From a letter to Padraic Colum; quoted by Damon, *Amy Lowell*, 564.

14. Lowell used different kinds of lines in "The Statue in the Garden," mostly alternating between rhymed couplets and free verse, to give the poem both an eighteenth-century and a modern atmosphere. See Damon, *Amy Lowell*, 564.

15. See preface to *Legends*, x–xi; and Damon, *Amy Lowell*, 535. Lowell's source for "Many Swans" is Franz Boas, *Kathlamet Texts*, Bureau of American Ethnology, Bulletin 26 (Washington, D.C.: Government Printing Office, 1901), 26–33.

16. A ladder of arrows reaches from earth to a country in the sky in the first of the tales recorded by Boas (*Kathlamet Texts*, 12). The same tale also refers to "a basket filled with human eyes" (ibid., 15)—a possible source for the same image in Lowell's early poem, "The Basket"?

17. Lowell's religious attitudes and her defense of her one explicit reference to Christianity, in the line "And a poison leaf from Gethsemane," are given in Damon, *Amy Lowell*, 560–61.

18. Padraic Colum, "A World in High Visibility," *Freeman* 4 (14 September 1921):18.

19. Quoted in Damon, *Amy Lowell*, 570.

Chapter Six

1. See Florence Ayscough's introduction to *Fir-Flower Tablets* in *The Complete Poetical Works of Amy Lowell*, 328. Edna B. Stephens discusses the influence of Oriental paintings on Fletcher and his interest in the haiku, in *John Gould Fletcher* (New York: Twayne Publishers, 1967), 57–65.

2. G. R. Ruihley quotes "Ombre Chinoise" as an instance of Lowell's "remarkable" sensitivity to "the emotional import of material forms." See his introduction to *A Shard of Silence: Selected Poems of Amy Lowell* (New York, 1957), xiv.

3. Damon, *Amy Lowell*, 506.

4. Frazer, *The New Golden Bough*, 134–35, 185.

5. Gould, *Amy*, 123.

6. Ibid., 82, 352. Clement Wood, *Amy Lowell*, (New York, 1926), notes that Lowell identified with the masculine role and point of view much more often than with the feminine in her love poems, and he virtually calls her a lesbian: "The tendency in the whole of the love poetry points over-poweringly to the conclusion that her attitude lies between that of Sappho and that of a masculine lover" (172). The self-loathing in "Sultry" could of course result from Lowell's identifying with Hermes, a male lover, and from the guilt and shame caused by his revelation to her of her own masculine leanings.

7. Gould, *Amy*, 356.

8. The lines are from Shakespeare's sonnet 73, "That time of year thou mayst in me behold."

9. The Hopkins phrase is from "To seem the stranger lies my lot, my life."

10. G. R. Ruihley, *The Thorn of a Rose: Amy Lowell Reconsidered* (Hamden, Conn., 1975), 175.

Chapter Seven

1. *New York Times*, 14 May 1925, 18.

2. Ferris Greenslet, *The Lowells and Their Seven Worlds* (Boston, 1946), 391.

3. Untermeyer, *The New Era in American Poetry*, 137.

4. The two references to Scott are to "Amy Lowell After Ten Years," *New England Quarterly* 8 (September 1935):321–22; and "Amy Lowell of Brookline Mass.," in *Exiles and Fabrications* (Garden City, N.Y., 1961), 117–18.

5. Untermeyer, *From Another World*, 123.

6. Untermeyer, *The New Era in American Poetry*, 140, 149; and *From Another World*, 124.

7. See Ruihley, *The Thorn of a Rose*, 11.

8. Flint, *Amy Lowell*, 21.

9. Horace Gregory, *Amy Lowell: Portrait of the Poet in Her Time* (New York: 1958), 212–13.

10. C. David Heymann, "Amy Lowell: The Last of the Barons," in *American Aristocracy: The Lives and Times of James Russell, Amy, and Robert Lowell* (New York, 1980), 239.

Selected Bibliography

PRIMARY SOURCES

A complete chronological listing of the first printing of poems and prose by Amy Lowell can be found in Damon, *Amy Lowell*, 729–42 (see below).

1. Poetry: Individual Books
A Dome of Many-Coloured Glass. Boston: Houghton Mifflin, 1912.
Sword Blades and Poppy Seed. New York: Macmillan Co., 1914.
Men, Women and Ghosts. New York: Macmillan Co., 1916.
Can Grande's Castle. New York: Macmillan Co., 1918.
Pictures of the Floating World. New York: Macmillan Co., 1919.
Legends. Boston: Houghton Mifflin, 1921.
Fir-Flower Tablets. Boston: Houghton Mifflin, 1921. With Florence Ayscough.
A Critical Fable. Boston: Houghton Mifflin, 1922.
What's O'Clock. Boston: Houghton Mifflin, 1925.
East Wind. Boston: Houghton Mifflin, 1926.
Ballads for Sale. Boston: Houghton Mifflin, 1927.

2. Poetry: Collections
Selected Poems of Amy Lowell. Edited by John Livingston Lowes. Boston: Houghton Mifflin, 1928.
The Complete Poetical Works of Amy Lowell. Introduction by Louis Untermeyer. Boston: Houghton Mifflin, 1955. A good working text, but not quite complete; it omits the "Phantasms of War" and all of Lowell's prefaces except that to *Fir-Flower Tablets.*
A Shard of Silence: Selected Poems of Amy Lowell. Edited by G. R. Ruihley. New York: Twayne Publishers, 1957.

3. Prose
Six French Poets: Studies in Contemporary Literature. New York: Macmillan Co., 1915.
Tendencies in Modern American Poetry. New York: Macmillan Co., 1917.
John Keats. 2 vols. Boston: Houghton Mifflin, 1925.
Poetry and Poets: Essays by Amy Lowell. Boston: Houghton Mifflin, 1930.

SECONDARY SOURCES

1. Bibliography

Kemp, Frances. "Bibliography of Amy Lowell." *Bulletin of Bibliography* 15 (1933–34):8–9, 25–26, 50–53. A selective, annotated list of books and articles by and about Lowell; helpful for locating some of the early Lowell criticism.

2. Books About Lowell

Damon, S. Foster. *Amy Lowell: A Chronicle.* Boston: Houghton Mifflin, 1935. A comprehensive biography and the chief source of information about Lowell—an indispensable book.

Flint, F. Cudworth. *Amy Lowell.* Minneapolis: University of Minnesota Press, 1969. Pamphlet length (45 pages), but a good objective summary of Lowell's life and writings.

Gould, Jean. *Amy: The World of Amy Lowell and the Imagist Movement.* New York: Dodd, Mead & Co., 1975. A good modern biography, containing material not available to Damon.

Gregory, Horace. *Amy Lowell: Portrait of the Poet in Her Time.* New York: Thomas Nelson & Sons, 1958. Stresses Lowell's conservatism and considers her poetry to be negligible; does provide insights into her literary milieu.

MacNair, Harley Farnsworth, ed. *Florence Ayscough and Amy Lowell: Correspondence of a Friendship.* Chicago: University of Chicago Press, 1945. Chiefly letters between Lowell and Ayscough about the writing of *Fir-Flower Tablets*—an important book.

Ruihley, Glenn Richard. *The Thorn of a Rose: Amy Lowell Reconsidered.* Hamden, Conn.: Archon Books, 1975. The first serious book-length criticism of Lowell's poetry; stresses her transcendental qualities and the influence of Zen Buddhism.

Wood, Clement. *Amy Lowell.* New York: Harold Vinal, 1926. A hostile, disparaging book that does, however, contain some sound criticism.

3. Articles and Parts of Books

Aiken, Conrad. "The Technique of Polyphonic Prose: Amy Lowell." In *Scepticisms: Notes on Contemporary Poetry,* 115–25. 1919. Reprint. Freeport, N.Y.: Essay Index Reprint Series, 1967. A harsh but discriminating analysis of *Can Grande's Castle.*

Aldington, Richard. *Life For Life's Sake: A Book of Reminiscences.* New York: Viking Press, 1941. Gives a firsthand account of the formation of the imagist movement and Lowell's part in it (133–49).

Bedford, William C. "A Musical Apprentice: Amy Lowell to Carl Engel." *Musical Quarterly* 58 (October 1972):519–42. Quotes and discusses important letters from Lowell to Engel.

Belmont, Eleanor Robson. *The Fabric of Memory*. New York: Farrar, Straus & Cudahy, 1957. Contains reminiscences of Lowell, especially of her later years, by a close friend (185–201).

Boynton, Percy H. "Amy Lowell." In *Some Contemporary Americans: The Personal Equation in Literature*, 72–88. Chicago: University of Chicago Press, 1924. Effectively refutes some of the exaggerated claims Lowell made for polyphonic prose.

Coffman, Stanley K., Jr. *Imagism: A Chapter for the History of Modern Poetry*. Norman: University of Oklahoma Press, 1951. A good objective discussion of the imagist movement, with a chapter on "Amygism."

Fletcher, John Gould. *Life Is My Song: The Autobiography of John Gould Fletcher*. New York: Farrar & Rinehart, 1937. Contains many memories and impressions of Lowell by one of her chief associates in the New Poetry.

Gerber, Philip L. "Dear Harriet . . . Dear Amy." *Journal of Modern Literature* 5 (April 1976):233–42. A lively account of the quarrelsome relations between Lowell and Harriet Monroe.

Greenslet, Ferris. *The Lowells and Their Seven Worlds*. Boston: Houghton Mifflin, 1946. Biographies, by one of Lowell's editors, of her and important members of her family.

Healey, Claire. "Amy Lowell Visits London." *New England Quarterly* 46 (September 1973):439–53. Uses important Lowell letters to discuss the quarrel between Lowell and Pound.

Heymann, C. David. "Amy Lowell: The Last of the Barons." In *American Aristocracy: The Lives and Times of James Russell, Amy, and Robert Lowell*, 157–279. New York: Dodd, Mead & Co., 1980. Gives a well-balanced view of Lowell's life, with stimulating insights into her personality and poetic goals.

Hughes, Glenn. *Imagism and the Imagists: A Study in Modern Poetry*. Stanford: Stanford University Press, 1931. Contains a history of imagism and separate chapters on leading imagist poets, including Lowell.

Lowes, John Livingston. "The Poetry of Amy Lowell." In *Essays In Appreciation*, 159–74. Boston: Houghton Mifflin, 1936. An intelligent assessment of Lowell's work, stressing her spirit of adventure.

MacLeish, Archibald. "Amy Lowell and the Art of Poetry." *North American Review* 221 (March 1925):508–21. An important review of Lowell's poetry—defends its essentially artistic quality.

Monroe, Harriet. *A Poet's Life: Seventy Years in a Changing World*. New York: Macmillan Co., 1938. The autobiography of the founder of *Poetry* and an important friend of Lowell's—with numerous references to Lowell.

————. "Amy Lowell." In *Poets and Their Art*, 78–85. New York: Macmillan Co., 1926. An estimate in which Lowell is said to have everything but poetic genius.

————. "Memories of Amy Lowell." In *Poets and Their Art*, 246–51. An affectionate obituary.

Overmeyer, Janet. "Which Broken Pattern?—A Note on Amy Lowell's 'Patterns.' " *Notes on Contemporary Literature* 1, no. 3 (May 1971):14–15. Argues that the speaker had agreed to her fiance's proposal of a natural, rather than a legal, marriage.

Perkins, Elizabeth Ward. "Amy Lowell of New England." *Scribner's Magazine* 82 (September 1927):329–35. Memories of Lowell by a lifelong friend.

Precosky, Donald A. " 'Make Ezra and the Whole Caboodle of Them Sit Up': Florence Ayscough and the Lowell-Pound Feud." *Four Decades of Poetry, 1890–1930* 2 (July 1979):204–9. On Lowell's use of *Fir-Flower Tablets* as part of her campaign against Pound.

Rittenhouse, Jessie B. *My House of Life: An Autobiography*. Boston: Houghton Mifflin, 1934. Gives a first-hand account of Lowell's appearances before the Poetry Society of America (256–70).

Rollins, Hyder Edward, and Parrish, Stephen Maxwell. *Keats and the Bostonians*. Cambridge: Harvard University Press, 1951. Includes the story of Lowell's dealings with Fred Holland Day for the use of his Keats manuscripts; with numerous letters by and to Lowell.

Schwartz, William Leonard. "A Study of Amy Lowell's Far Eastern Verse." *Modern Language Notes* 43 (March 1928):145–52. Traces the growth of Lowell's interest in and use of oriental art forms.

Scott, Winfield Townley. "Amy Lowell of Brookline, Mass." In *Exiles and Fabrications*, 114–23. Garden City, N.Y.: Doubleday & Co., 1961. A summing up of Lowell's life and work which questions if she was a poet at all.

Sedgwick, Ellery, III. " 'Fireworks': Amy Lowell and the *Atlantic Monthly*." *New England Quarterly* 51 (December 1978):489–508. Discusses—using letters—the often stormy relationship between Lowell and Ellery Sedgwick, the conservative editor of the *Atlantic Monthly;* a good article.

Self, Robert T. "The Correspondence of Amy Lowell and Barrett Wendell, 1915–1919." *New England Quarterly* 47 (March 1974):65–86. Letters between Lowell and Wendell, a senior Harvard professor, about Lowell's work and methods.

Sergeant, Elizabeth. "Amy Lowell: Memory Sketch for a Biographer." In *Fire Under the Andes*, 11–32. New York: Alfred A. Knopf, 1927. A friend's account of Lowell's manner of living and working.

Taupin, René. *L'Influence du Symbolisme Francais sur La Poésie Américaine (de 1910 a 1920)*. Paris: Libraire Ancienne Honoré Champion, 1929. An informative study of the French influence on imagism; Lowell discussed in detail, though not very favorably (166–92).

Tupper, James. "The Poetry of Amy Lowell." *Sewanee Review* 28 (January 1920):37–53. A sensible analysis of Lowell's poetry through *Can Grande's Castle.*

Untermeyer, Jean Starr. *Private Collection.* New York: Alfred A. Knopf, 1965. Memories of the New Poetry years, including several important incidents involving Lowell (74–89).

Untermeyer, Louis. "Amy Lowell." In *The New Era in American Poetry,* 137–59. New York: Henry Holt & Co., 1919. An enthusiastic appraisal of Lowell at the height of her career.

_____. "Storm Center in Brookline." In *From Another World: The Autobiography of Louis Untermeyer,* 99–125. New York: Harcourt Brace & Co., 1939. Lowell's personality as seen by a close associate, whose estimate of her work fell considerably after her death.

Williams, Ellen. *Harriet Monroe and the Poetry Renaissance: The First Ten Years of Poetry, 1912–22.* Urbana: University of Illinois Press, 1977. A good account of the Lowell-Pound-Monroe relationship (129–45).

Index

DATE DUE

GAYLORD			PRINTED IN U.S.A.